THE MOST INCREDIBLE FOOTBALL STORIES OF ALL TIME FOR YOUNG READERS

TRUE INSPIRATIONAL TALES ABOUT PERSEVERANCE AND COURAGE TO INSPIRE YOUNG FOOTBALL LOVERS

JORDAN ANDERS

CONTENTS

INTRODUCTION

Football isn't just any old sport. It's a game that grabs our attention, runs with it, and doesn't let go!

One of my favorite things about football is its surprises. Whether it's your favorite team making a comeback in the playoffs, or one of your favorite players scoring a long-shot touchdown, there have been countless classic football moments throughout NFL history that people still remember just like they happened yesterday. This, for me, is why football is the greatest game; because every moment is an opportunity to witness on-field magic.

Football, of course, is also about being part of a team—even if you're in the stands or watching from home. Rooting for the 49ers was a big part of my childhood, and my dad ruled the remote every Sunday, of course, and anytime Monday Night Football was on.

The feeling I get today when my team scores still feels the same as it always did. As a fan for so long, it truly feels like I did it too! In this way, it's not just the players who are part of the team. Everyone watching is participating, part of a big football family, tailgating, cheering, and celebrating together.

Football isn't just about athleticism and dodging those big tackles on the field; it teaches us some important lessons about life. Football shows us how working together can make us better and that being strong and brave can help us tackle any challenge we encounter—not just in sports, but in life too!

Even though the game of football has been threatened by some tough things, like various controversies, or arguments about rules or player safety, it's still the most-watched and one of the most beloved sports in America. That's because the game is constantly changing and getting better, making sure it's safe and fun for everyone from the little leagues up to the pros.

When we get together and watch football with our friends and family members, it becomes about much more than just the sport itself. It's about making memories, learning from the pros, and often, finding out that not everything's about winning. When we see our favorite team give it their best while getting hammered on the field, it's easy to see that the real magic of football isn't found just in victory, but realized through playing the game and being part of something bigger in front of tens of thousands of screaming football fanatics.

Football is an important part of American culture—along with baseball, it plays a part in American imagination, often finding its way into movies, commercials, and our daily conversations. From the Friday night lights of high school football games across the country to gathering around the TV every Sunday during football season, families and friends share together in the excitement and suspense that each game brings. It's a tradition that of course extends to holidays like Thanksgiving, where the game is as much a part of the celebration as the turkey on the table. Super Bowl Sunday, of course, is a holiday in its own right for many of us football die-hards!

The game itself is a spectacle of physical might and strategic genius, where players execute plays that require both athletic skill and sharp mental acuity. It's like chess, but with real people instead of pawns, rooks, and knights. The unpredictability of football, where any team can win on any given day, adds to the thrill and keeps us glued to the game.

Whether it's a last-second touchdown or a surprising play, football never fails to deliver excitement. Even beyond the field, the sport lives on through fantasy football leagues, where football fans across the country are able to participate in the excitement out-of-season, managing their own teams and competing with friends, which keeps the spirit of competition alive all throughout the year.

Above all, football is a unifying force, bringing together Americans of all ethnicities, ages, and backgrounds under one flag. The game days, tailgating parties, conversations and arguments about favorite teams, and memorable plays all lend themselves to a sense of community that goes way beyond the sport itself.

This book is all about exactly that: the football community, and the heroes who made it possible for people from all different walks of life to come together over this unique game. As we start taking a look at the stories of football's greatest legends, we see common themes of resilience, teamwork, and determination, the effects of which often spread far beyond the gridiron. The stories of America's football legends inspire us, reminding us that with passion and perseverance, anything is possible.

My aim in putting together this book is to inspire you, young readers and football fans across the nation, by telling you the true stories of these remarkable athletes. Their stories aren't just about attaining excellence in the NFL; they're about overcoming obstacles, standing strong when things don't turn out right, and working hard in every aspect of life.

As you flip through these pages, you'll encounter stories of players who were able to spin challenges into triumphs. You'll read about players like Jim Brown, who didn't just dominate the field as an all-time legend, but also stood up for civil rights when he wasn't playing. We'll also look at more recent stars, like Peyton Manning, whose preparation and perseverance made him a legend. Even living legend Tom Brady had to find his way through tough times before he reached the top. Though he was a late draft pick, this never kept him from becoming one of the most celebrated quarterbacks in NFL history. Players like Drew Brees, who returned from what could have been a career-ending injury to break multiple records, show us the importance of never giving up on your dreams.

Each story gives us insider access into the lives of 21 football legends who haven't just left their mark on the sport but also on the world. These tales will show you that heroes come in many forms and that true greatness often takes more than just talent. It requires heart, hard work, and a strong will to push beyond the limits in every way.

I invite you, young reader, to see yourself in these stories. Think about your own dreams and the challenges you face in life, at home, or in school. How can the qualities of these legends—like their determination, teamwork, and integrity—help you define your path and pursue your passions?

I'd like to ask that you crack open the pages of this book with an open heart and a curious mind. Be ready to be inspired, to laugh, to learn, and to be motivated. These stories aren't just about football; they're about the game we call life, and how to play it with courage, passion, and strength, like our favorite players approach the game on-field. So, get ready to dive in and be part of something bigger than yourself. Join me on this exciting adventure and discover how you, too, can become a football great both on and off the field!

Chapter 1

TOM BRADY

You have to believe in your process. You have to believe in the things that you are doing to help the team win. I think you have to take the good with the bad.

—TOM BRADY

Tom Brady has been called the "GOAT" (Greatest Of All Time) by many football experts, as well as by tons of regular kids like you. His story shows us the power of self-belief and how our determination to succeed in life can turn our limitations into legendary achievements. Though you might be limited to playing tag football at recess these days, if you work really hard, who knows? You might just make it to the top like Tom did!

Born in San Mateo, California, Brady's journey from being a regular sports-obsessed kid just like you to becoming one of the most iconic figures in sports is nothing short of inspirational, showing us that anything is possible!

Brady's career was so good that it challenged the way football experts normally look at career record-setting and statistics. Aside from his sky-high stats and all the records he set, his on-field dedication to being the best shows us the value of preparation and mental toughness.

Tom Brady's desire for excellence and his pledge to live up to that standard in every way was ultimately what allowed him to stay cool under pressure, and led him to achieve unparalleled success in the NFL, including seven Super Bowl victories and numerous all-time records. Through Tom's story, we can learn to see challenges as opportunities for growth and to never underestimate the power of believing in ourselves. Let's tackle the story of Tom's life and see how he made his way to football greatness!

TOM'S STORY

Tom Brady's entry into the NFL was far from glamorous. Drafted 199th overall in the 2000 NFL Draft, his road to NFL fame is a quintessential underdog story. He was the sixth-round draft pick for the New England Patriots, and his skills on the field were overshadowed at first. The thing was, the Pats already had a star QB: Drew Bledsoe.

Brady, at first, was overlooked, and his skills on the field were really underestimated. It wasn't until later that it would be his time to shine. In the next few years, he would undergo a dramatic transformation, from a doubted prospect to an NFL superstar!

Brady's rise to the top really kicked off in 2001 when Drew Bledsoe was on the bench with an injury. This was just the opportunity Brady was looking for. He knew it was his time to prove himself.

While Bledsoe was recovering, Brady became the starting QB. He wasn't just a "good enough" replacement—he actually managed to bring the Patriots to their first Super Bowl victory in 2002! This marked the start of a new era for the team and put Brady's skills on full display!

Over two decades with the New England Patriots, Brady carved out a legacy of on-field dominance, leadership, and success. Under the guidance of coach Bill Belichick, Tom Brady led the Pats to six Super Bowl titles, repeatedly proving his ability to excel on the sport's biggest stage. His time with the Patriots really managed to redefine the organization, making them one of the best NFL teams in history!

In a move that shocked the sports world, and sports fans all over the New England states, Brady left the Patriots in 2020 to join the Tampa Bay Buccaneers. With the Buccaneers, Tom simply chose to drown out the sounds of all the naysayers and led them to a Super Bowl victory. Though some New England sports fans were mad at him for leaving their team, his Super Bowl win with the Bucs proved to everyone that he was able to lead teams to victory no matter where he went.

Throughout his entire career, Brady shattered numerous NFL records, and he currently holds titles for most career wins, touchdown passes, and passing yards. His record-breaking performances give future generations of QBs a lot to live up to. Brady's legendary status is backed up by his seven Super Bowl wins—an achievement that beats out every other player in NFL history, not to mention his five Super Bowl MVP awards! These achievements highlight his consistent excellence in high-pressure games and his role in some of the most memorable moments in NFL history.

Known for his remarkable comebacks, Brady has engineered some of the most dramatic reversals in football, including the historic comeback in the 2017 Super Bowl against the Atlanta Falcons. His mental toughness and ability to perform under pressure have earned him the moniker "the Comeback King."

Ignoring the typical career arc of NFL quarterbacks, who can get worn out or sloppier as they get older—Brady continued to set records well into his 40s, becoming the oldest QB to win a

Super Bowl and to also be named MVP. His longevity and peak performance have challenged conventional beliefs about aging in professional sports.

Off the field, Brady has done a lot of charity work and community leadership. He has contributed lots of money to different charitable causes, making sure that his football success has had an impact that goes far beyond the gridiron, and showing the world that his leadership qualities can have a positive impact on society, not just the sports world.

After announcing his retirement in 2023, the impact of Brady's career continues to be felt across the NFL and sports culture at large. Known for his compelling comebacks, his great plays, and his leadership on the field, Brady remains one of the greatest quarterbacks in history, leaving a legacy that goes way beyond the records he broke and the Super Bowl rings he earned.

TOM BRADY FUN FACTS

- At the University of Michigan, Brady was mostly a backup, and ended up sitting on the bench a lot, a stark contrast from the later success he found as the most vital element of his team.
- Brady was obsessed with maintaining his sharpness on the field, even trying out memory-boosting techniques most often used by people facing dementia or neurological problems to improve his reflexes and analytical skills on the field.
- Brady is the only quarterback to have Super Bowl wins that span three different decades!
- Football wasn't Tom's only sport. Did you know he was drafted to the Major League Baseball team the Montreal Expos?

THINGS TO THINK ABOUT

- How does the fact that Brady was a backup QB in college and in his first seasons in the NFL challenge the idea that we have to have success right away? What's an example of something that you got better at the more you practiced it?
- What can you learn from Brady's dedication to his craft and his ability to perform under pressure and have amazing comebacks?
- How does Brady's charity work make his life story go far beyond his achievements in football, and show that he cares about the world and not just sports?

UP NEXT

As we conclude our exploration of Tom Brady's remarkable journey—a story of defying odds and setting new standards in the NFL—we now turn our attention to another transformative figure in football: Walter Payton!

Known for his record-setting career, Payton's work ethic and charity work earn him high marks from football fans who have a heart. In his story, we see that there are plenty of players in football who decided to apply their talents off the field too!

Chapter 2

WALTER PAYTON

If you start something, you shouldn't quit; that is what we were taught. If you're going to play, you might as well play to be your best.

–WALTER PAYTON

Known affectionately as "Sweetness" for his smooth playing style and kind demeanor, Walter Payton's path toward football greatness from a small town in Mississippi all the way to the NFL is a tale of extraordinary dedication and talent. Throughout his career with the Chicago Bears, he didn't just set records and get a Super Bowl ring— he also won hearts with his strong work ethic and giving nature.

Like many of the star athletes in this book, life wasn't just about football for Walter when he was a kid. His early passions for both music and sports helped him develop a well-rounded personality that he could use to achieve greatness both on and off the field. As we take a closer look at his story, we'll discover the depth of his character and the impact he had on the world of football and beyond!

WALTER'S STORY

Born in Columbia, Mississippi, Walter was born into a family that cared about sports. His dad had even played minor league baseball at one time, though his main job was working hard in a factory to support his family. Walter had two siblings growing up, and he grew up playing Little League baseball and participating in the Boy Scouts.

By the time he was in high school, he was really into playing the drums in the school marching band. Later, he became a talented drummer playing jazz fusion. Even once he got into football, his passion for music never faded, showing us that it's okay to be interested in many things. We never have to pick just one interest to focus on!

After graduating from high school, Walter attended Jackson State University. There, he shone on the football field and set a new team record for rushing touchdowns, showing everyone that he had natural talent and could one day make it to the pros. NFL scouts started to notice his playing, and in 1975, he was selected fourth overall by the Chicago Bears in the NFL Draft—the beginning of what would come to be a legendary 13-season career.

In his first NFL season, he really didn't play that well until the final game of the season against the Saints. He didn't let this slow start deter him, however, and the next season he started to become a star! During his time with the Bears, Walter broke numerous records, including ones in rushing yards gained, and he became famous for his "stutter-step," a unique way of stop-and-start running that became his signature.

His talents on the field were on full display during the 1985 Super Bowl, where he played a really big role in leading the Chicago Bears to victory in Super Bowl XX. Off the field, Walter was known for his incredible work ethic, leadership, and generosity, traits that won him points with fans and teammates alike.

Walter's contributions to football were recognized by his getting inducted into both the Pro Football Hall of Fame and the College Football Hall of Fame. He also had the honor of being named to the All-Time Team list of best players in NFL history twice, for both the 75th and 100th anniversary of the NFL's founding. Beyond his stellar football skills, Walter was known as a humanitarian at heart, starting the Walter and Connie Payton Foundation, raising awareness for organ donor programs, and helping give toys to poor kids at Christmas.

Walter's namesake, the Walter Payton Man of the Year Award, which the NFL gives out every year to the player who does the best work off the field, helps us remember his deep commitment to serving his own community after he retired.

After retiring from pro football, Walter faced a really big setback that he battled with as much courage as he showed on the field as a running back. Toward the end of his life, he battled cancer that was caused by a rare liver disease.

Walter sadly passed away in 1999, but he remains an eternal inspiration for football fans across America. Today, he's still remembered as much for his on-field achievements as for his "sweet" character, his humility, and his "do-good" nature.

Walter's motto was "Never die easy," and he certainly did not, going out fighting until the last minute.

WALTER PAYTON FUN FACTS

- Walter's nickname first became "Sweetness" because of his smooth playing style on the field.
- Walter set a single-game rushing record by running for 275 yards against the Minnesota Vikings in 1977, beating O.J. Simpson's

previous record. And the craziest thing was that he had the flu, and was suffering from a bad fever during that record-setting game (Weyer, 2022)!

- His career rushing total reached 16,726 yards, a record that was considered unbreakable for over 20 years, until it was eventually broken by Dallas Cowboys running back Emmit Smith (Weyer, 2022).
- Walter played in 186 games in a row, only missing one game in his rookie year (*Walter Payton*, 2021a).

THINGS TO THINK ABOUT

- How does Walter Payton's early interest in music show us that we can do all kinds of things, not just sports?
- What can you learn from Payton never missing a game after his rookie season and breaking a rushing record while he was sick with the flu?
- How does Payton's influence extend beyond football? Did you know that lots of grown-ups register as organ donors today, partially due to star athletes like Walter who battled rare diseases?

UP NEXT

As we reflect on the life of Walter Payton, a hero who was taken from us too soon, it's time to turn our attention toward another awe-inspiring tale. Next, we'll be learning the story of Jerry Rice, whose legendary career in the NFL set new standards for dedication, performance, and success.

Like Payton, Rice wasn't just known for the records he set, but also for his unique playing style. Jerry Rice in fact is considered by many to have revolutionized the way the wide receiver position is played, and his life story stands as yet another thrilling chapter in the legacy of football's greatest players. So, let's turn the page and learn about how Jerry Rice changed the game and the world for the better!

Chapter 3

JERRY RICE

I think the thing about that was I was always willing to work; I was not the fastest or biggest player but I was determined to be the best football player I could be on the football field and I think I was able to accomplish that through hard work.

–JERRY RICE

From a small town in Mississippi to packed NFL stadiums, Jerry Rice's journey to becoming the all-time leading receiver is a story of impressive perseverance and dedication to the sport. When Jerry was a kid, he wasn't even that into sports, but that didn't stop him from becoming a star athlete once others recognized his natural talent.

It wasn't until he was in high school that others saw Jerry's natural speed and agility while he was cutting out of class early one day. Instead of punishing him for trying to play hooky, the school principal saw that he might be great at football if only he were to focus his energies toward the sport.

Jerry Rice went far beyond his modest upbringing and his lack of experience as a youth athlete, showing us that with great determination and hard work, we can become star players even if we don't get started in sports until we're already in our teenage years. So, let's take a look at the story of a star player who not only broke records but also set new standards for what it means to achieve and redefine the game.

JERRY'S STORY

Born the son of a bricklayer, hard work was a part of Jerry's upbringing. He was a small-town boy who grew up in a family where breaking a sweat was just a part of life. Though he liked to play with all the other kids, there was one thing that set Jerry apart from others; he could run faster and harder than they ever could.

After getting caught by the school principal, Jerry learned that all his natural talents could be focused toward something, and all he had to do was work really hard. Jerry wowed the whole school with his amazing football skills, and college scouts began to notice.

So, off he went to Mississippi Valley State, a place where he would have the opportunity to shine on the field and in the classroom. There, he was part of what was called the "Satellite Express," along with fellow star player Willie "The Satellite" Totten, he set numerous NCAA records. By the time he graduated, Rice held records for receptions, receiving yards, and touchdown receptions.

Even though he played great during college, Rice wasn't a top pick during the 1985 NFL Draft. The San Francisco 49ers (go team!) recognized that he had great potential though, and drafted him 16th overall. The 49ers' decision to take Jerry Rice into their fold would end up being one of the best draft picks in NFL draft history, as he'd go on to become a legend.

Rice's first season as a pro was challenging though. He dropped a few passes and felt like there was so much pressure to perform that it was impossible to think or play well. He'd made it to the pros, but he was struggling at first. Then, something happened, and he was quickly able to turn all that potential within him into on-field excellence. Soon enough, he was smashing NFL records.

He went on to play for a staggering 20 years where he redefined what it meant to be a pro wide receiver. Over his entire career, he broke NFL records for receptions, receiving yards, and touchdown receptions. His record of 1,549 receptions over his career and his accumulation of 22,895 receiving yards were unprecedented and set a new benchmark for future generations of NFL players (*Jerry Rice Biography: NFL Football Player*, 2024).

Rice's playoff performances are still remembered by football fans today. He played in four Super Bowls, winning three. In Super Bowl XXIII, he was named MVP after catching 11 passes for 215 yards and a touchdown, one of the greatest efforts by any single player ever in Super Bowl history, and a record he still holds today (Allen, 2024).

After spending many seasons with my home team the 49ers, Jerry went on to play for the Oakland Raiders and for a short time the Seattle Seahawks too. Even as he started to get older, he continued to play at a high level, showing everyone that age was just a number.

When he finally decided to retire from the NFL, Jerry Rice was widely recognized as one of the greatest to ever play the game. His records and impact on the game endure to this day.

JERRY RICE FUN FACTS

- Jerry Rice was famous for his rigorous training regimen, which included running up the steepest hills of San Francisco!
- Jerry's talents on the field were recognized repeatedly. He was named to the Pro Bowl 13 times and earned first-team All-Pro honors 10 times (*Ten Fun Facts about Jerry Rice*, n.d.).

- In the strike-shortened 1987 NFL season, Jerry Rice received an astonishing 22 touchdown passes in just 12 games (Allen, 2024).
- Jerry's Super Bowl records are equally impressive, holding the highest number of receiving yards in a single Super Bowl, which he set the record for in 1989 against the Bengals (*Most Receiving Yards in a Single Game in Super Bowl History*, n.d.). He was also the only player to have caught three touchdown passes in a Super Bowl two times (Fawkes, 2024).
- Throughout his career, Rice had a great dynamic with two star Hall of Fame quarterbacks, Steve Young and Joe Montana. He caught 67 touchdown passes from Montana and a record 92 from Young (DeArdo, 2023).
- Rice is the only wide receiver to have earned Pro Bowl honors after turning 40.

THINGS TO THINK ABOUT

- How did Jerry Rice's upbringing and the discovery of his athletic talent in high school shape his work ethic and approach to football?
- What can you learn from Rice's transition from having a less-than-perfect rookie season to becoming the greatest wide receiver of all time?
- How does Jerry's career show us the importance of perseverance and dedication?

UP NEXT

As we've seen, Jerry Rice's dedication and record-setting achievements have certainly left a mark on the NFL, with his amazing playing and his many records that remain unbroken today!

Next up, we'll take the story of another monumental figure in football history. Turning our attention to Peyton Manning, we'll meet a star QB whose strategic thinking and on-field leadership reshaped the quarterback position.

Manning's career didn't just redefine offensive play—it also set new benchmarks for future generations in the sport. So, come along, and let's find out how the legend himself Peyton Manning's innovative approach and commitment to excellence made him a star!

Chapter 4

PEYTON MANNING

There are other players who were more talented, but there is no one who could out-prepare me.

–PEYTON MANNING

Born into a family with a strong legacy of football greatness, Peyton Manning carried the torch passed down by his father, Archie, and played alongside his brother, Eli, and had a big impact on the sport.

From his early days throwing perfect spirals at Isidore Newman School in New Orleans to shattering records at the University of Tennessee, and onto a legendary NFL career with the Indianapolis Colts and Denver Broncos, Peyton's journey was one of extraordinary achievements and inspiring leadership.

Peyton Manning's legendary work ethic, strategic play creation, and leadership skills on the field led his teams to multiple victories, while also earning him a place as a true icon in the world of football.

PEYTON'S STORY

Growing up in a household that lived and breathed football, Peyton absorbed a lot about the game from his dad and carried the family's pro football legacy from his high school days growing up in New Orleans up until he finally got drafted.

Peyton's football career can be traced back to his school days at Isidore Newman School in New Orleans. There, he dominated the field while also showing teammates and coaches his leadership skills. In high school, he led his team to an impressive record and set the stage for his future success.

By the time he was ready to go off to college, he was a star player and had many offers from different schools. He decided to play for the University of Tennessee. There, he broke numerous school records and set new standards for the team. His amazing throwing arm strength, accuracy, and understanding of the game made him a standout college football star, paving his way toward eventual NFL stardom.

The 1998 NFL Draft was a huge turning point for Manning's career, as he was the first-round draft pick for the Indianapolis Colts and the first overall. Peyton now had a huge task in front of him. He was expected to add a new sense of vigor to the franchise while also fulfilling the demanding roles expected of star quarterbacks. He knew that with the Colts, he'd have to play with lots of preparation and apply all the football intelligence he'd spent his whole life building.

Manning was put in as the starting QB for the Colts right away. He had a pretty rough rookie season and didn't do so great, but he had bursts of pure excellence in his playing that were a sign of the great things to come. His ability to learn from the mistakes made in each game and his dedication to the sport and to continuing his family's legacy set the foundation for what would become a legendary career.

Over his entire football career, which lasted 18 seasons, Manning shattered tons of NFL records, including most passing yards and touchdown passes in a season. His great passing skills and the ability to craft complicated plays made him one of the top QBs in the league.

Peyton's career was largely defined by the legendary performances he made in high-stakes games, bringing the Colts to a victory in the 2006 Super Bowl and earning MVP honors. After departing from the Colts, he continued his success with the Denver Broncos, winning a second Super Bowl at the end of the 2015 season, showing everyone that he was truly one of the game's greats.

Known for his incredible leadership, and his ability to rally together teammates from all different backgrounds and playing styles, Manning was also a role model off the field. His community service efforts were recognized when he was awarded the Walter Payton NFL Man of the Year in 2005.

Though Manning's career was defined by his outstanding plays, it wasn't without its own challenges. He had many injuries that threatened to knock him off-track, one of which he needed to get a potentially career-ending neck surgery for. Peyton stayed strong throughout rehabilitation, and he managed to return to the field with the Broncos, continuing onward against all odds.

Peyton made the tough choice to retire after his second Super Bowl win, rather than keep playing and risk damaging his body further. It had already been almost 20 years since he got drafted, and he knew it was finally time to hang up his cleats. When he retired, he had already been recognized as one of the greatest quarterbacks in NFL history.

His exceptional teamwork and strategic on-field skills as a QB have changed the game forever, setting the stage for the star quarterbacks of today, who can only attempt to live up to the new standards he set.

PEYTON MANNING FUN FACTS

- Peyton won a staggering five NFL MVP awards over his career!
- Known for his skills in analyzing the other teams' defense, his ability to see what they were planning gave him a strategic upper hand. The moves he made pre-snap were based on these keen observations and led to his stellar performance.
- Manning was the first starting NFL quarterback to win a Super Bowl with two different teams, with the Colts in 2006, and with the Broncos to cap off the 2015 season.
- He currently holds the record for the most passing touchdowns in a single season, having had a staggering 55 in 2013 alone (*NFL Passing Touchdowns Single-Season Leaders*, n.d.).
- Manning is famous for his "Omaha" pre-snap call.
- Over his career, Manning made 14 Pro Bowl appearances (*Peyton Manning*, n.d.).
- Manning's Peyback Foundation has provided more than $13 million through various grants and programs, showing his dedication to giving back to the community (*Walker, 2017*).

THINGS TO THINK ABOUT

- What qualities do you think Peyton showed with his teammates that made him a good leader, and how can you apply leadership skills to your life within your peer group?
- What does Peyton Manning's comeback from neck surgery teach us about resilience and determination?
- How has Peyton's legacy in football changed the game and how people think about the quarterback position?

UP NEXT

As we close the page on Peyton Manning, it's time to look at the story of another star QB whose impact on the sport is equally profound.

The next chapter is all about Jim Brown! Let's get ready to learn about what made him one of the best players ever!

Chapter 5

JIM BROWN

There is no excuse for violence. There is never a justification for anyone to impose themselves on someone else. And it will always be incorrect when it comes to a man and a woman, regardless of what might have happened. You need to be man enough to take the blow. That is always the best way. Do not put your hands on a woman.

—JIM BROWN

Jim Brown's words show us that being strong isn't just about physical power; it's also about standing up for what's right and treating others with respect.

As I mentioned in the book Introduction, Jim Brown wasn't just famous for his amazing skills in football—he became widely known for the courage he showed, the courage to speak up for fairness and kindness, both on and off the field. His life story is packed with exciting sports action and important lessons about helping others and doing the right thing.

Jim may have run fast on the football field, but it's the hard work he did to make the world a better place that made him a legend. We'll see how he used his fame to help others and stood strong for justice, inspiring many young players like you along the way. So, let's peer into the life of this incredible athlete and hero.

JIM'S STORY

Born on St. Simons Island, Georgia, Jim faced some tough times right from the start, as the South was still rife with racism and discrimination against African Americans. His dad was out of the picture by the time baby Jim was just two weeks old, and soon after, his mother moved to New York to find work. Jim was placed in the care of his kindly great-grandmother, and he wouldn't get to know his mom at all until a little bit later.

When Jim was eight years old, he finally got reunited with his mother. Newly relocated to New York, Jim began to show what he was made of, overcoming early life challenges and the racism he faced there, too. While New York was a big city in Yankee country, Jim realized that hate knew no borders from a very young age and that African Americans faced a lot of discrimination in Northern states too, not just back home.

Jim's mom got a place in Long Island, and he was enrolled at Manhasset Secondary School. Once he got to his new school—Jim didn't just play football; he also played other sports, including track, basketball, and even lacrosse. His talent at sports was undeniable, and his drive to be the best was clear from the start. Football, though, was where he did best, blazing through defenses and setting the stage for an even brighter future in college.

Once he graduated from high school, Jim went off to Syracuse University. There, he continued to dominate on the football field while also still playing lacrosse. Despite facing racial barriers at Syracuse, he became a standout athlete, breaking records and earning the respect of teammates and opponents. His college years were a mix of challenges and success on the field. As he showed off his talent and mental toughness, it was time to start thinking about his next move, one that would see him move up to the pros!

Drafted by the Cleveland Browns, Jim quickly became the best in the league, leading in rushing yards multiple times. His strength and speed were impressive to his coaches and teammates alike. His ability to change the direction of a game in the Browns' favor was something that fans and players could only marvel at. But then, right at the peak of his career, Jim did something unexpected—he retired. Fans were shocked.

Jim decided it was time to do something else in life. He had made it to the top, but in his heart, he knew he had to go in another direction. He decided that he was going to focus on acting and civil rights activism. Transitioning into a successful acting career, he became one of America's first African-American action-hero movie stars, breaking barriers in the film industry, just as he had on the football field.

Rather than just bask in all the on-screen success he had, Jim decided it was time to make a big change in his life again. He was going to use all the attention he was getting for an important cause: equal rights for all! Jim began to push for social change, becoming an advocate and activist for civil rights and greater economic opportunities for African Americans. He understood the power of his voice and his responsibility to use it to fight for justice and equality, and that's just what he did!

As founder of the Amer-I-Can program, Jim made it his life's work to empower young African American youth and promote education, self-esteem, and social responsibility. His founding role in this organization showed the world his commitment to making a positive impact on society, and everyone could see that he was a true hero.

Today, Jim Brown isn't just remembered as a great football player, but also for his civil rights and community service efforts. His history of helping others rise up shows us just how much one person can achieve with some talent, lots of hard work, and a strong will.

JIM BROWN FUN FACTS

- There's a bronze statue of Jim standing outside the stadium that the Cleveland Browns play in. It has been standing since 2016.
- Jim has been officially recognized as one of the greatest 100 players of all time by the NFL, an honor he received in 2019.
- When he played, Jim Brown led the NFL in rushing yards in eight of the nine seasons he played in (CNN Editorial Research, 2023).
- Jim never missed a single game throughout his entire NFL career.
- When Jim became a movie star, he acted in some famous films, including the World War II flick *The Dirty Dozen* and the Western films *Rio Conchos* and *100 Rifles*.
- Jim earned the All-American honors in Lacrosse while studying and playing football at Syracuse. He's also in the National Lacrosse Hall of Fame for his achievements in that sport!
- In 2023, Jim passed away, and to honor his legacy, the NFL renamed its league rushing title to The Jim Brown Award.

THINGS TO THINK ABOUT

- How did Jim Brown's parents leaving him in his great-grandmother's care when he was young help him learn toughness, and later achieve success both on and off the field?

- What can Jim's transition from sports to acting and activism teach you about pursuing all different kinds of interests? What are the things you like to do besides football?
- How does Jim's story inspire you to overcome hurdles in life and stand up for what you believe in?

UP NEXT

From learning Jim Brown's story, we can really see the power of perseverance, the importance of using one's voice for good, and the courage to blaze new trails. Jim showed us that challenges on and off the field can be transformed into stepping stones for success and platforms for advocacy. His path from a challenging childhood to a sports icon and a voice for civil rights shows us that we can do more than just sports—we can actually make meaningful changes in the world!

As we turn the page, it's time to get ready to explore the life of another football great, Michael Strahan.

Chapter 6

MICHAEL STRAHAN

The great thing coming from sports is you understand the concept of a team. It leaves no room for being selfish, and that's something I picked up from home.

–MICHAEL STRAHAN

Michael Strahan's story shows us how teamwork, adaptability, and charisma can lead to success both on and off the field. Raised in a military family, Strahan learned early on the importance of discipline and teamwork, values that he carried into his career in the NFL.

Michael was a latecomer to the sport and didn't start playing until he was in high school. Once he got hooked on football though, it soon became clear to everyone that he had the makings of a star. He didn't end up just becoming an NFL force, as he also became a charismatic media personality.

All in all, it's Strahan's big personality and energy that helped him transition from a celebrated athlete to a beloved television host, offering valuable lessons on the importance of embracing change and keeping all the options open in his career and life.

MICHAEL'S STORY

Michael grew up in Houston, Texas, but his life changed big time when his family took him to live in Germany. He was an army brat, and his time spent on the military base where his dad worked would prove to be highly influential, but not in ways that led to him becoming a star athlete. That would all happen later.

Football, as it turned out, was the favorite sport in Germany, but "football," Michael learned, is what they call soccer in Europe! Whatever these sports were called in the different places Michael lived in as a kid, he didn't know too much about any of them; that was, until Michael's family moved back to Texas. By that time, he was already a senior in high school! He didn't know the first thing about the game, but that didn't stop him from trying out for the team.

Michael was a big guy and was really into weightlifting at the time. Since he was so powerful, everyone knew he'd make a great addition to the team even though he didn't know the first thing about football. Michael got picked for the high school team, and he was a quick learner. He didn't just make up for lost time and prove his merit during that season—he actually managed to get a football scholarship to Texas Southern University!

At Texas Southern, Michael dominated the field, setting school records and earning All-America honors. His amazing performance at this lower-tier school drew the attention of NFL scouts, showing his ability to stand out from the rest despite his school not being a Division 1 team.

The New York Giants were really impressed with Strahan's skills, and they ended up selecting him in the second round of the 1993 NFL Draft. This choice marked the beginning of what would be a legendary professional career in football and broadcasting.

Michael didn't necessarily shine in his first few seasons, but everyone knew him as a great guy, and he had a unique ability to get along with all kinds of people, maybe from all his time spent living in a foreign country. Though he wasn't a star on-field right off the bat, he stuck with it and steadily improved. His breakout year came in 1997, earning him his first Pro Bowl selection. Not only was he developing a more complex understanding of the game—he was really starting to shine!

Known for his ability to sack quarterbacks like no other, Strahan became one of the NFL's premier defensive ends. He wasn't a huge guy compared to other defensemen in the league, but his strength and strategic play made him a great asset for the Giants.

In 2001, Strahan set the NFL single-season sack record with a total of 22.5 sacks, showing his skill and tenacity (Augustyn, 2024a). This record is a highlight of his career and was a big step in carving out his legacy.

The pinnacle of Strahan's NFL career came when he led the Giants to a victory in the 2007 season's Super Bowl, overcoming the previously undefeated New England Patriots in a historic upset! Strahan made the tough choice to retire that season, right after his big win. All in all, he had made 141.5 career sacks, a Giants franchise record (*Michael Strahan*, 2021). His departure from professional football marked the end of an era for the Giants. Michael's football greatness was officially recognized when he got inducted into the Pro Football Hall of Fame in 2014.

After his retirement, it was time for Michael to think about his next step. He decided to use the charisma he showed on the field to entertain TV audiences all over the country. Strahan was successful in launching a second career in broadcasting, soon becoming a beloved media personality.

Michael appeared in shows like "Good Morning America" and "FOX NFL Sunday," gaining praise from fellow TV personalities and cheers from his fans who followed his path to fame all the way from his not-so-impressive NFL debut to his big moment of Super Bowl glory.

But being a big TV star wasn't enough for Michael; he knew he wanted more out of life, and had more to offer the world. He became a business entrepreneur and even ended up writing a book! He launched his own line of men's clothing in 2015, and published his best-selling book, *Wake Up Happy*, that same year. All his non-football-related passions in life show us the broad range of interests we can all have as athletes. It doesn't all have to be about the game.

Michael Strahan's story isn't one that's just about sports; it's one about getting started much later than most players, working hard to get good at the game, then eventually breaking records, and then doing much more than just football. Michael's path from the football fields of his high school to the big TV of New York, shows us his charm, charisma, and ability to excel at all kinds of things.

MICHAEL STRAHAN FUN FACTS

- Strahan's charm and skill as a TV broadcaster have earned him multiple Daytime Emmy Awards.
- Aside from his well-known appearances on daytime talk shows, he has also been in movies and TV shows, including *Magic Mike XXL* and *Brooklyn Nine-Nine*.
- Michael's estimated net worth is over $65 million, making him one of the wealthiest former NFL athletes.

THINGS TO THINK ABOUT

- How does Michael Strahan not having played football until his senior year of high school change the way we think about natural talent and skill development in sports?
- What can you learn from Strahan becoming a TV star after retiring from professional sports?
- How does Strahan's work creating his own line of men's clothing show the importance of staying open to new ideas in life and business after sports?

UP NEXT

As we close the chapter on Michael Strahan, a figure whose slow-burn skills on the football field only became apparent well into his life, and a man who found his way to TV and business success—we transition to another inspirational athlete.

Our next chapter is all about Drew Brees, a quarterback known for his precision and skill on the field and for the big impact he made off it. Brees' story is one of perseverance and leadership, serving as a great role model for aspiring athletes and community leaders alike. Let's jump right into the story behind this grand champion of football and humanitarianism.

Chapter 7

DREW BREES

You can accomplish anything in life if you are
willing to work for it.

—DREW BREES

In the world of professional sports, few stories teach us more about the power of having faith and demonstrating leadership qualities on and off the field quite like that of Drew Brees.

Drew Brees' career arc stretches from some early challenges he faced as a youngster to pinnacle achievements both on and off the field. Drew Brees' meteoric rise, from an underdog to a champion, shows us the power of perseverance and positive leadership in the face of adversity.

Throughout his career, Brees has exemplified how challenges can be transformed into opportunities, setting a powerful example for young athletes like you, and for anyone aiming to make a meaningful impact in their community.

DREW'S STORY

Born in Austin, Texas, Drew Brees grew up in a family that was big on sports but had some problems. The divorce of his parents was hard for young Drew, but it gave him a toughness that later allowed him to overcome some big bumps in the road that threatened to derail his love of playing football.

The first major setback he faced was a serious ACL injury when he was in high school. Despite the difficult recovery from this injury, Brees' performance as a Texas high school football star earned him praise from local football fans and the press, but he still didn't get the attention of scouts. The reason why the top college teams weren't interested in Drew's skills wasn't because of his injury—they just thought that he wasn't big and strong enough and that his throwing arm wasn't powerful enough. Those who followed Austin-area high school football knew better, and they could see that he had what it took to make it to the pros.

Drew didn't care so much what the big colleges thought of his playing, and he knew he was good, so off he went to Purdue University to study Industrial Management, and of course to play football. While not one of the top college teams at the time, it was a Big Ten school and a place where Drew's football skills could shine. Once he got there, he was simply on fire. He shattered tons of records and proved to everyone who saw him play that he had what it took to make it to the top.

Drafted by the San Diego Chargers, Brees' early professional years were marked by initial struggles and eventual triumph. However, just as his career was ascending, a severe shoulder injury at the end of the 2005 season cast a long shadow over his future prospects in the NFL. Many wondered if he would ever throw a football with the same precision again.

In 2006, Drew signed with the New Orleans Saints, a team that at the time wasn't doing so well. The problem wasn't anything that happened during games—it was that all the players had to live through some traumatic moments, as one of the biggest natural disasters in American history swept through the city, devastating local communities that were plagued by an ineffective and slow government response. Hurricane Katrina changed a lot of things in New Orleans, and Drew Brees joining the Saints in a way represented a fresh beginning.

The city and the team were about to enter a new era, as they pumped out the water, cleaned up the streets, and remembered those who were lost in the terrible tragedy. Under Brees' leadership, the Saints experienced somewhat of a resurgence, all coming to a head with a victory at the Super Bowl for the 2009 season, where Brees was named MVP. This period with the Saints didn't just show football fans his skills as a quarterback—it also widened his ability to inspire others and unite a community that was still in recovery and mourning from the hurricane around their shared passion for the Saints.

Throughout his career in pro football, Drew Brees' name almost became synonymous with record-shattering. He set benchmarks with his impressive stats and set a few new records in completions and touchdown passes in a row. Each record he broke showed off his technical skills on the field, and drew attention to his consistent performance, which ended up spanning two decades!

Beyond the field, Drew's contributions to society have been meaningful. His charity work, especially after Hurricane Katrina, and ongoing community involvement have solidified his legacy as a person who cares not just about his team—but their city too. His efforts during the post-hurricane period showed selflessness and a deep commitment to rebuilding and supporting communities in need.

Choosing to retire after the 2020 season, Drew left behind a whole bunch of football and community service memories for the people of New Orleans and football fans across the country that go beyond the records he broke and his stats. Known for his leadership on the field, and his generous nature, Brees has inspired countless others to rise above the challenges at hand and go forward with courage.

DREW BREES FUN FACTS

- In the 2018 season, Drew Brees set the record for the highest completion percentage in a single season, completing an astonishing 74.4% of his passes (Shapiro, 2018).
- Over his career, Drew Brees set many NFL records, including the ones for most passing yards, most games-in-a-row where he had a touchdown pass, and completions (Cardona, 2024).
- Brees Dream Foundation is Drew's cancer research charity. His commitment to helping others earned him the Walter Payton NFL Man of the Year Award in 2006 alongside San Diego Chargers running back LaDainian Tomlinson.
- Drew wrote a book called *Coming Back Stronger* where he talks about overcoming adversity and turning setbacks into comebacks, just like he did when the injury in high school threatened to keep him off the field forever. It's one of my personal favorite books written by a football player, and is definitely worth reading!

THINGS TO THINK ABOUT

- How did Drew Brees turn his early career challenges into opportunities for growth and success later in life? Why do you think he wrote a book to share his experiences with others?
- What does Brees' work in the community after Hurricane Katrina teach us about the impact athletes can have off the field?

UP NEXT

As we turn the page on our look into Drew Brees' career, marked by his determination and will to overcome adversity both on and off the field, we shift to another inspiring figure in the world of football: Michael Oher!

Michael Oher's journey, characterized by lots of challenges and triumphs, is yet another compelling chapter in the story of football's greatest who have also made impacts beyond the game. Let's take a closer look at the life and career of Michael, whose story from hardship to NFL stardom has inspired millions of young players like you.

Chapter 8

MICHAEL OHER

Do what's best for you, and do it to the best of your ability - go after your goals like nobody's business.

–MICHAEL OHER

Few success stories in modern sports history, compare to Michael Oher's. His journey from the streets of Memphis to the bright lights of the NFL, depicted in the acclaimed film *The Blind Side*, offers more than just a narrative of personal success—it showcases the profound impact of kindness, mentorship, and never letting go of your dreams despite the obstacles.

This chapter is all about the life of Michael Oher, tracing his path through the challenges of his early life when he experienced neglect and instability, to his transformative years under the care of a kindly foster family, and onto his achievements in the high-pressure arenas of college and professional football. Each phase of his life offers unique insights into the power of believing in ourselves, the critical role of support systems, and the sheer force of will that can change the course of our fate.

MICHAEL'S STORY

Michael Oher's life story begins with hardship and instability. Born into tough circumstances in Memphis, Tennessee, Michael faced many adversities from a young age, most notably, a very tumultuous family life.

Michael's childhood was not a happy one, and he was shuffled around between different foster homes and schools. He was also homeless for some periods of time. He had no consistency, and no stable family life to help support him. Then, one day—something amazing happened. Michel was adopted by a family called the Tuohys. They were really nice and provided the stability and support Michel needed. He needed some kind of guidance in life if he was ever going to get out of the bad circumstances he was born into.

Despite all the pain, Michael knew it wasn't his fault that he was born into poverty and family problems. The Touhys sent Michael to Briarcrest Christian School, where he began to undergo a transformation. He went from being a street kid to being a football star! Even though Michael didn't have a lot of experience playing football, by the time he got to his senior year, he was wowing his coaches, teammates, and spectators with amazing plays.

But it wasn't just Michael's football skills that blossomed during this time—he also started making serious improvements with his schoolwork. With an incredible drive to succeed, he studied really hard, and was eventually able to get his GPA up high enough to reach the NCAA requirements for Division I scholarship eligibility.

By this time, college scouts had begun to take notice of Michael's playing, and suddenly he was one of the most sought-after recruits; all the big schools were interested in his talents. He had gone from being a homeless kid to being on the brink of a major life change, as he would be headed off to college to become a football star while pursuing his newly found academic goals too!

Michael went off to the University of Mississippi, where he became a star player on the legendary Ole Miss Rebels. He earned All-American honors and was considered to be one of the top players on the team. Some had doubted his abilities at first due to his size and background, but he showed everyone, including all the naysayers, that he had what it takes.

In 2009, something big happened: Michael's dream of playing professional football finally came true! He was the 23rd-round draft pick for the Baltimore Ravens. In his rookie season, he showed flexibility on the field, and his talent was undeniable. Coaches put him at various positions on the offensive line, and he quickly adapted to the demands of the professional game.

Michael's crowning achievement came when he played an important part in the Ravens' Super Bowl victory in the 2012 season. His performance during the game was crucial to the team's success. He had become one of the top players in the NFL. What a journey it had been from his rough upbringing to Super Bowl stardom!

After his time with the Ravens, Michael signed with the Tennessee Titans and later the Carolina Panthers. His career continued to be marked by personal breakthroughs as well as some new challenges, including dealing with a concussion that impacted his playing and his health.

Michael's personal and professional life was further brought into the public eye through *The Blind Side*, a film that was made based on a 2006 book by Michael Lewis that chronicled Michael Oher's life story. The big-screen version of Michael's life story brought widespread attention and inspired many football fans young and old.

Aside from playing football, Michael has been active in lots of charity work. His commitment to giving back to the world that granted him so much opportunity is driven by his personal experiences and a desire to improve the lives of others facing adversity and help them rise up.

MICHAEL OHER FUN FACTS

- Michael won the NFL's Ed Block Courage Award in 2009.
- Off the field, Oher has ventured into business opportunities and has appeared in front of audiences as a motivational speaker.
- Michael first tried for the 2008 NFL Draft but decided to finish school first. He entered the draft the following year and was selected by the Baltimore Ravens as their 23rd overall pick.
- Aside from the book about Michael Oher that the movie The Blind Side was based on, Michael wrote his own book called *I Beat the Odds*.
- Although the Tuohys considered themselves to be like adoptive parents to Michael, they never actually adopted him but instead had a conservatorship agreement with him. Today, the family and Michael remain in a prolonged legal battle over money received from *The Blind Side,* public speaking fees, and investment funds that Michael says he never received back from the family.

THINGS TO THINK ABOUT

- Despite the instability and challenges of his early life, Michael excelled in academics and sports once he got the right support he needed. What can we all learn from this?
- Michael Oher's journey challenges many stereotypes about people from troubled backgrounds. What does his story teach us about the dangers of preconceived notions and the potential that lies within all of us?

UP NEXT

As we turn the page from Michael Oher's inspiring journey of triumph against the odds, we transition to another compelling narrative that blends sports, heroism, and sacrifice.

The next chapter is all about the life of Pat Tillman, whose story from NFL stardom to military service encapsulates a profound dedication to principles and courage. So, let's lace up our boots and march forward into the story of a man who left the football field for the battlefield, showing us that sometimes serving the nation can be even more fulfilling than pursuing our own dreams on the football field.

Chapter 9

PAT TILLMAN

Somewhere inside, we hear a voice. It leads us in the direction of the person we wish to become. But it is up to us whether or not to follow.

—PAT TILLMAN

Of all the American heroes who risk their lives to defend our country, only a select few leave professional sports careers behind to join the ranks. Pal Tillman is one of these brave sports stars. In the wake of the September 11 attack, he decided to leave football behind forever and trade his cleats in for a pair of combat boots.

This chapter is all about the life of Pat Tillman, focusing on his extraordinary dedication to living with integrity and purpose. From his formative years to his rapid rise in college and professional football, and his subsequent enlistment in the U.S. Army, Tillman's story is a compelling exploration of sacrifice and patriotism, teaching us an important lesson about making decisions according to our values. As you'll see, Pat wasn't just a public hero—he was also known as a kind man who was dedicated to his family, his teammates, and his fellow soldiers.

PAT'S STORY

Pat Tillman's story is one that's about the pursuit of dreams and about having a sense of duty. Born in San Jose, California, Tillman grew up in a tight-knit family, which laid the foundation for his strong character and beliefs. From an early age, his athletic skills were clear to everyone. The football skills he showed in high school got him a scholarship at Arizona State University.

Once at Arizona State, Pat's profile on the football field continued to grow. He led the Sun Devils to an undefeated season and a trip to the Rose Bowl, earning the Defensive Player of the Year title in the Pac-10 conference. Off the field, Pat was a great student, completing his marketing degree with a 3.85 GPA (*Remembering Pat Tillman at Arizona State: A Great Sun Devil, a Greater Man*, 2024).

After college, Pat finally had a chance to play in the NFL. He was drafted by the Arizona Cardinals, where he quickly became a starting safety. Known for his integrity, he famously turned down a really big contract that he was offered by the St. Louis Rams, instead choosing to show his loyalty and dedication to the Cardinals rather than earn more money.

Though Pat was doing well with the Cardinals, his life changed dramatically following the events of September 11, 2001. Deeply moved by the attacks, Tillman made a decision that stunned many: He turned down a $3.6 million contract extension to enlist in the Army alongside his brother, Kevin, who also wanted to serve the country (Biography.com Editors, 2017). In the Army, Pat continued to demonstrate his leadership and courage, completing Ranger School and serving tours in Iraq and Afghanistan.

Tragically, Pat's life was cut short in 2004, when he was killed by friendly fire in Afghanistan—an incident that was at first covered up by the military. Having a high-profile sports star get killed by a fellow U.S. soldier did not make the Army look good, especially since the mission in Afghanistan was not clear. Pat's unfortunate passing sparked a national controversy and a deep investigation into the circumstances of the incident.

After he lost his life in Afghanistan, Tillman was honored with the Silver Star and Purple Heart, and his legacy continues to influence through initiatives like the Pat Tillman Foundation, which supports veterans and their spouses with academic scholarships.

The foundation created in Pat's honor hopes to make sure his spirit and values live on, offering things like scholarships to military veterans and their spouses who share Tillman's commitment to service, learning, and action.

Hopefully, this will make people realize that Pat's story isn't defined by the tragic way he died, but by how he lived—a life marked by courage, passion, and an unyielding commitment to making a difference.

Pat Tillman's journey from the football fields of Arizona to the rugged landscapes of Afghanistan is a poignant narrative of sacrifice and service, though he died not at the hand of a foreign enemy, but by a fellow brother in arms. His life story shows us that we should live life by our own principles, even if it means putting ourselves in harm's way.

PAT TILLMAN FUN FACTS

- Standing at 5' 11", some considered Pat a bit too small to be a linebacker, but he soon proved all the naysayers wrong (McLaughlin, 2017).

- Pat graduated Summa Cum Laude from Arizona State in just 3 1⁄2 years (Fish, n.d.).
- Pat was voted "most masculine" in his high school graduating class.
- Though Pat was known as a true patriot and was inspired to go to Afghanistan after 9-11, he spoke against the "illegal and unjust" U.S. war in Iraq (McGreal, 2009). Pat even had plans to meet with leftist agitator Noam Chomsky upon his return from his tour of duty, but he never made it back to do so.
- Some have accused the U.S. Department of Defense of staging a cover-up over Pat's death.

THINGS TO THINK ABOUT

- What does Pat Tillman's decision to leave the NFL for military service and his willingness to criticize the U.S. government teach us about what patriotism and sacrifice really mean?
- What lessons can you learn from Pat's dedication to his principles, regardless of the fact that they cost him his life?
- How can Pat's legacy encourage kids across America to serve and contribute to their communities and country? What are some things you can do to help out if you care about the country besides going to war?

UP NEXT

From the inspiring story of Pat Tillman, whose courageous choices redefined heroism in the modern age, we transition to another monumental figure in football: John Madden!

Known not just for the video game named after him or his coaching mastery—Madden was one of football's greats because he changed how fans engage with the sport. Madden's legacy, like Tillman's, goes far beyond the gridiron.

As we turn the page from Tillman's story of ultimate sacrifice and steadfast values, get ready to learn about how Madden's innovations and passion for football have left a mark on the game and the football community.

Chapter 10

JOHN MADDEN

*Self-praise is for losers. Be a winner. Stand for
something. Always have class, and be humble.*

–JOHN MADDEN

John Madden's path to football fame, from an aspiring football
player in Minnesota to becoming one of the most iconic figures in
NFL history, is a story of passion, perseverance, and, above all, a
deep reverence for the game.

Madden's influence on the game goes way beyond his Super Bowl-win-
ning season as a coach and his pioneering career as a broadcaster.
He singlehandedly transformed how millions of fans understand and
interact with football, bringing the game straight into their living
rooms as if the players were jumping out of the screen!

Madden's career was built on more than just strategy and play-calling;
it was also built on a foundational commitment to education, in-
novation, and genuine respect for the sport. Through his legendary
commentary, transformative coaching, and of course, as the namesake of the Madden NFL video game, John Madden taught us that
football isn't just a game—it's something that demands passion,
knowledge, and humility. John's story shows us that football isn't
just like any other sport; it's a way of life.

JOHN'S STORY

John Madden was born in Austin, Minnesota, but his family ended up moving to Daly City, California. It was there that he became a high school football star. This early period set the stage for his lifelong commitment to football, laying a solid foundation for his future success in the NFL.

Madden's high school football skills led him to the College of San Mateo and then later to Oregon, before he finally settled at Cal Poly, San Luis Obispo. He soon got drafted by the Philadelphia Eagles! Just as he finally made it though, his football dreams were cut short. He got a terrible knee injury at training camp, making his entry into the pros a bit tricky. He definitely didn't want to be benched all the time—he didn't know what to do!

This setback could have been the end for John Madden. What did he do, however? He turned his misfortune into a big opportunity, and instead of playing, he started coaching. This big event in his life, one that really could have spelled the end of his career, actually turned out for the best. This was all due to his hard work and positive attitude. By turning what could have been a career-ruining injury into an opportunity, John Madden set the stage for future success.

It's not like they just let him become coach or even assistant coach for the Eagles though; he basically had to start at the bottom, by taking a humble coaching role at Allan Hancock College. He did so well there, that he was able to quickly move onto better opportunities, becoming a defensive assistant at San Diego State under Don Coryell.

His innovative defensive strategies and charisma at San Diego State led him to the Oakland Raiders, where he became the linebackers' coach in 1967 and then the head coach by 1969, making him the youngest head coach in the AFL/NFL at the time.

Under Madden's leadership, the Raiders flourished. During his time there, the Raiders never had a losing season, and they ended up winning the Super Bowl for the 1977 season. His coaching style might have been a bit different from what other coaches were doing at the time, but his approach to player management and game strategy worked, and he started to gain lots of attention for his innovative techniques.

By 1979, everyone knew John Madden's name—but something started to change. He just couldn't handle it anymore. He cared too much about football, and he realized that if he didn't take a break, he wouldn't be able to do a good job anymore. His health was starting to suffer. John Madden made the difficult decision to step down from his coaching role. But guess what? He wasn't leaving the game for good; instead, he was going to make a big change in his life—just like he did when he got injured right after getting drafted. John Madden was going to become a sports broadcaster!

Making the transition from the sidelines to the TV broadcasting booth was a big change, but Madden met the challenge head-on like he did with everything in life. Teaming up with Pat Summerall, Madden's voice became synonymous with NFL broadcasts, bringing his deep knowledge of the game to life with his enthusiastic and easy-to-understand style of explaining plays.

Madden's likability and his straightforward style made him a national star. In 1988, he was asked to get involved in a new project that would come to be one of his most successful pivots yet. He was going to have a video game named after him!

Electronic Arts (EA) founder Trip Hawkins got in touch with Madden, knowing that the only way to make a realistic football simulation was to have the game done with the advice of someone who had an amazing understanding of the game.

Trip wanted to make a game that mirrored an actual NFL lineup, which meant 11 players per side and a real playbook. John Madden's expertise and insistence on authenticity pushed the developers to innovate beyond the technical limitations of the time. The game was successful, and the John Madden Football franchise lives on, still being played on today's modern computers and gaming consoles.

John Madden passed away in 2021 and is still one of the most recognized names in football.

JOHN MADDEN FUN FACTS

- John Madden was afraid of flying in planes, so he always rode around in a bus called the "Madden Cruiser."
- When John became the coach of the Oakland Raiders at age 32, he became the youngest head coach in NFL history.
- John's work as a sports broadcaster won him a total of 16 Emmy Awards (Angeles, 2024)!

THINGS TO THINK ABOUT

- How did John Madden's injury that kept him from playing football lead him to find his true calling in coaching and broadcasting? What's an example of something you used to like to do, that you turned into some other pursuit or hobby?
- What does Madden's move from coaching to broadcasting tell you about adapting to change and always looking for new opportunities?

- How has the Madden NFL video game franchise affected the way people view and interact with football today?

UP NEXT

John Madden's ability to blend deep knowledge with infectious enthusiasm opened up the complexities of football to a broader audience, making the game more accessible and enjoyable for all.

As we continue to think about Madden's influence on football, it's time to look at the life story of another standout figure known for his athleticism and vibrant personality: Rob Gronkowski!

Chapter 11

ROB "GRONK" GRONKOWSKI

You've just got to have to put the work in. Put work first. Put the hours in and the time in, and do your job. And when you get a little time off, you can go out and have a little fun. But you have to make sure you get done what you need to get done first off.

–ROB GRONKOWSKI

Rob Gronkowski, also known as "Gronk," shows us all how to work hard and have fun at the same time. He believes that if you focus on doing your best work first, there's always time to enjoy yourself after. From his early years in New York, all the way to becoming a superstar in the NFL, Gronk has always put a lot of effort into everything he does while making sure to enjoy life as much as he can!

His story isn't just about being great at sports. It's also about being a fun person who makes everyone smile, even when we're just watching football on TV. In this chapter, we'll learn how Gronk combined serious dedication with a fun-loving attitude to become one of the best tight ends in football history. Whether he was setting records on the field or making people laugh off it, Gronk's story teaches us about the importance of hard work, staying strong through tough times, and having a good time along the way.

GRONK'S STORY

From his early days in Amherst, New York, Gronk showed a profound passion for sports, growing up in a family where athleticism was a common thread. He did really well in football, basketball, and hockey during his high school years, but it was on the football field where he truly made his mark, earning honors at the state level and within the state All-Western division for his fierce playing as a tight end and defensive end.

Gronkowski's great playing led him to the University of Arizona, where, despite undergoing back surgery that shortened his college career, he set school records for a tight end and earned All-American honors. His college performance managed to catch the attention of NFL scouts, and in 2010, he was the second-round draft pick for the New England Patriots.

Gronk quickly rose to stardom in the NFL, where he was recognized as much for his ability to make big plays as he was for his rock-solid blocking. His record-setting performances included setting the record for the most receiving touchdowns in a single season by a tight end in 2011, which established him among the game's elite (*Rob Gronkowski Has the Most Receiving Touchdowns by a Tight End in a Season, with 17 Touchdowns in 2011*, n.d.).

His NFL career included multiple Super Bowl championships, where he contributed countless plays that led both the Patriots and later the Tampa Bay Buccaneers to victory. Gronkowski briefly retired in 2019 but returned to the NFL to join former teammate Tom Brady in Tampa, adding yet another Super Bowl title to his resume. After retiring officially in 2021, Gronkowski left behind a legacy as one of the greatest tight ends in the history of the sport.

Off the field, Gronk's larger-than-life personality has endeared him to fans worldwide. Known for his community work and charitable efforts, he even created an organization called the Gronk Nation Youth Foundation, an organization that helps young athletes like you reach their potential through sports, education, and fitness.

Gronk isn't just a great athlete; he also co-authored a best-selling book and runs a fitness equipment business. He has also become a familiar face through various media appearances, showcasing his playful nature on talk shows and reality television, making him a true cultural icon.

Since retiring from professional football in 2022, Gronk has even dipped his toes into professional wrestling with the WWE. His post-retirement activities not only highlight all the various interests he has besides football but also reflect his continuous drive to maintain a strong connection with fans and followers, making every endeavor a new playing field for his unbounded energy and enthusiasm. Gronk's story shows us that the game itself is important, but that we should also have fun!

GRONK FUN FACTS

- Gronk comes from a family of athletes, with his brothers and father all having sports backgrounds themselves.
- Gronk loves music, and he even started his own music festival called the Gronk Beach Party! The 2024 lineup for his Big Game Weekend is set to include performances by Flo Rida, Afrojack, and DJIrie.

THINGS TO THINK ABOUT

- How did Gronkowski's early athletic experiences across multiple sports contribute to his success in football?
- What qualities helped Gronkowski overcome injuries and setbacks throughout his career?

- How can you draw inspiration from Gronkowski's dedication to both his professional career and charitable work?

UP NEXT

As we turn the page from the remarkable story of Rob Gronkowski, whose exuberant personality and commanding presence on the field charmed fans, it's now time to take a look at another dynamic and transformative figure that's rocked the NFL over the last few seasons: Patrick Mahomes!

Known for his groundbreaking playing style and leadership, Mahomes continues to redefine the quarterback position and inspire a new generation of athletes. Let's explore how one of today's hottest NFL superstars is shaping the future of football as we know it!

BE A HERO!

Heroes are ordinary people who make themselves extraordinary."

— GERARD WAY

Isn't it incredible that heroes can be from any area of life? When you think about heroes, you probably first think of superheroes, and then maybe you think of firefighters or doctors – people who save lives. They're all heroes, it's true, but so are these brilliant footballers. As you know by now, it's not about the touchdowns or field goals they score… It's about the challenges they've faced and the determination they've shown to get where they are.

Are you feeling inspired? You should be! You can be a hero too, and with all these amazing stories in the back of your mind, you're going to be reminded of what determination, resilience, and commitment can bring you… Whatever it is you want to achieve, those qualities will get you there.

We'll get back to our footballers in a moment, but before we do, I'd like to ask you a favor. I'd like to ask you to inspire more young readers like yourself and share these stories with them too. How? Well, you could tell your friends about this book, or you could talk about what you've learned here when you're at school… or you could go one better and reach even more people by writing a review online (or asking your parents too!).

By leaving a review of this book on Amazon, you'll spread these amazing stories and inspire more young people to follow their dreams.

You could say you're being a hero simply by talking about these remarkable people and sending so much inspiration out into the world!

Thank you for your help. Now, let's get on with our next incredible story.

Scan the QR code below

Chapter 12

PATRICK MAHOMES

I feel like, even if something goes wrong, I have confidence in myself and my team that we'll fix it.

–PATRICK MAHOMES

Patrick Mahomes's approach to football and life reflects a confident, joyful spirit, one that doesn't shy away from challenges but meets them head-on. Mahomes definitely has leadership qualities, wants to be the best player he can, but also likes to have fun doing it!

PATRICK'S STORY

Born in Tyler, Texas, into a family already very well accustomed to the world of professional sports, Mahomes has always been destined to make an impact. With a father who played Major League Baseball, it's no surprise that Patrick inherited his dad's natural athletic talent and a great sense of sportsmanship.

From his early days, Patrick's skills have wowed onlookers. By the time he got to high school, he wasn't just a great football player, he played baseball and basketball too! This early sign of Patrick's versatility put all different kinds of skills he had to the test, and the natural sense of leadership he demonstrated hinted at the great things to come. By the time he was ready for college, he knew it was time to focus and get down to work.

Patrick knew he had a tough decision ahead of him. Though he knew he was a football star-in-the-making, he loved baseball too, and he wanted to make his dad proud. He decided to stick with both sports and see what happened.

At Texas Tech, he became an important member of the Red Raiders, leading their NCAA division in touchdowns and passing yards. Patrick knew it was time to make a tough choice; the Detroit Tigers drafted him in 2014, and he had to think hard about whether he really saw a future for himself in baseball. He decided that even though he got drafted by an MLB team, he was doing so well at football with the Red Raiders, it was time to leave baseball behind. It was time to hone his craft and have a chance at the NFL.

Three years later, Patrick's NFL dreams came true! The Kansas City Chiefs drafted him as the 10th-round pick. Mahomes spent his rookie year under the mentorship of Alex Smith—a year that was characterized by lots of learning and hard work.

By 2018, Patrick was put in as the Chiefs' starting quarterback; he was simply phenomenal. His breakout season was marked by an incredible performance, getting both MVP and Offensive Player of the Year honors. But this was just the beginning. Patrick helped bring The Chiefs their first Super Bowl win in 50 years! He was offered a record-breaking $503 million contract extension in 2020—the largest in sports history at that time (Patra, 2020)!

Patrick's playing style is characterized by incredible arm strength, mobility, and a flair for making the seemingly impossible plays possible. He doesn't just entertain fans on the field while delivering great plays—what he's really done is that he's brought a fresh perspective to the way the quarterback position is played. Through his innovative approach, he's setting the wheels in motion for future QBs to pick up the reigns and continue to redefine the way the position is played in the next few decades.

Off the field, Mahomes is just as impactful. His involvement in various charitable causes and commitment to community and youth development shows us that he's a star athlete who's deeply aware of his ability to influence and inspire beyond the game.

After seeing some unfair things happening in the world, like when George Floyd was killed by the police, Patrick and some of his football friends decided to make a video. They wanted the NFL to help stop racism and make things fair for everyone. Patrick also helps with More Than a Vote, a group started by basketball star LeBron James to ensure everyone can vote and have their say.

Besides speaking up, Patrick loves to help kids through his own charity, the 15 and the Mahomies Foundation. This foundation works hard to improve life for kids who need a little extra help. Patrick doesn't stop there—he's also part owner of the Kansas City Royals in baseball and Sporting Kansas City in soccer, showing his love for all sports. Plus, he always finds time to promote products he believes in and even made it to the list of Time magazine's 100 Most Influential People in 2020. Patrick shows us that being a sports star is also about helping others and having a big heart!

PATRICK MAHOMES FUN FACTS

- Patrick loves to put ketchup on all his food. He was even asked to be a spokesperson for Heinz ketchup!
- His nickname, "Showtime," was created by his dad who always supported his interest in sports.

- Patrick has a huge collection of sneakers. He's got over 180 pairs, including some really rare ones (Lakritz & Kalnitz, 2024).
- Patrick played so well in the 2018 NFL season that he landed on the cover of the Madden NFL video game the next year!

THINGS TO THINK ABOUT

- How do you think Patrick's multi-sport background made him such a great quarterback?
- How do you think Patrick's playing style is different to how other star QBs play the position?
- How does Patrick's commitment to community and supporting social causes inspire you to give back to your own community?
- Would you like to have as many pairs of sneakers as Patrick? Or do you think he has too many?

UP NEXT

As we turn the page on the story of Patrick Mahomes, we've now seen how he made his way from a multi-sport high school star to becoming an NFL legend. His innovative playing style and commitment to his community haven't just changed the way we see other NFL quarterbacks play, but they've also set a new standard for leadership in sports.

Now, as we leave Patrick's story behind us, it's time to turn our attention to another iconic name in NFL history—Jim Kelly. Kelly was another player whose leadership both on and off the field left a mark on the world of football. So, get ready to learn about the life and career of this legendary player as we peer into the challenges and triumphs that came to define his legacy!

Chapter 13

JIM KELLY

Make a difference today for someone who's fighting for their tomorrow.

–JIM KELLY

From his early days as a high school quarterback to his legendary NFL career and courageous personal battles, Jim Kelly's story isn't just about football greatness, it's also about the strength of the human spirit. As we explore his life and legacy, we'll discover how he turned adversity into opportunity, inspiring others to never give up, no matter the odds stacked against them.

JIM'S STORY

Born in Pittsburgh, Pennsylvania, Jim grew up to become a high school football sensation at East Brady High School, where his skills as a quarterback dazzled all who watched him play. With a truly amazing 3,915 passing yards and 44 touchdowns, his high school career set the stage for his future successes in college football and the NFL (*College Days: Jim Kelly*, n.d.).

Despite an initial setback where Penn State wanted him as a linebacker, Jim was set on being a quarterback. He ended up going to the University of Miami, where they were willing to put him in as

QB. At the University of Miami, Jim thrived, setting several records and securing his place in the university's Hall of Fame. His playing during college caught the attention of professional scouts, not from the NFL, but from USFL, another professional league that existed for a brief period of time in the 1980s. Jim became a standout player for the USFL team the Houston Gamblers, earning MVP honors.

Jim's NFL journey began when he reluctantly joined the Buffalo Bills after the USFL didn't make it further than the 1985 season. Overcoming his reservations about the cold weather he'd encounter in upstate New York, he helped lead the team into a new area of success, including four Super Bowl appearances in a row, from 1991 to 1994—an NFL record! Throughout his NFL career, Jim racked up some impressive stats, broke numerous records, and was recognized with multiple Pro Bowl selections and an All-Pro honor.

Off the field, Jim was facing some really tough personal challenges, including his son's battle with Krabbe disease and his own fight against a rare form of jaw cancer that he was diagnosed with in 2013. Pat chose to make his battle with cancer public and showed his fans and followers strength and vulnerability. Kelly underwent multiple surgeries and rounds of chemotherapy and radiation, always sharing his journey with transparency and hope with others as he battled the disease, inspiring and giving hope to others facing similar battles.

These battles tested his strength and character but also inspired football fans across the nation, many of whom had similar struggles in their families. Inspired by his personal experiences, Jim established the Hunter's Hope Foundation, dedicating his efforts to giving back and supporting other families dealing with illnesses.

Jim stayed strong, and he beat cancer in 2014! His work helping kids with rare diseases like the one his son has isn't the only way he's lending a helping hand these days. Jim is also very involved in motivational speaking, where he often discusses the importance of perseverance, faith, and the power of community support. His annual football camp for youth, for example, doesn't just operate as a sports clinic, but also as a platform for mentoring young athletes like you about the value of hard work, discipline, and teamwork.

Jim Kelly's life story is about much more than the Bills' Super Bowl streak or the records he set; it's about his ability to still smile despite all the problems life throws at us. That's what really set Jim apart from other players; not only did he show leadership both on and off the field, but he showed everyone that he had a real commitment to making a difference in the lives of others, and inspired them to do the same. Jim was inducted into the Pro Football Hall of Fame in 2002 for his impact on the game.

JIM KELLY FUN FACTS

- Jim Kelly set a massive record by throwing for 574 yards in one game, the most ever in a professional football game in the United States (*Feb. 24, 1985: Jim Kelly Throws for 574 Yards with Houston Gamblers*, n.d.)!
- Jim holds the Buffalo Bills' records for most passing yards, touchdowns, and completions.
- He became famous for the rapid-fire "K-Gun" offense technique, which didn't allow the opposing team any time to get their defensive plays together.

THINGS TO THINK ABOUT

- As we learned, Jim runs his own football camp. Would you like to go one day?

- How did Jim Kelly's determination to play quarterback shape his career path from college to the NFL? What's an example of a time when someone told you you should do something different than your dream and you pursued it anyway?
- What qualities did Jim exhibit that made him a leader on and off the field?
- How can the way Jim dealt with personal and professional challenges inspire you in facing difficulties?

UP NEXT

As we close the chapter on Jim Kelly, whose courageous battles on and off the field have left an indelible mark on fans and players alike, we prepare to explore another story of football success.

The next football star we'll be learning about is Steve Gleason, a player whose journey through personal adversity has not only tested his spirit but has also transformed it into a powerful force for societal change. Like Jim Kelly's, Gleason's path to football fame was one of incredible strength and determination, showing the world how challenges can lead to impactful and lasting contributions to society.

Chapter 14

STEVE GLEASON

I have moments where I miss my old self. But I think anyone can get caught up in what we used to have. But at the same time, we can choose to focus on the beauty of now.

—STEVE GLEASON

Steve Gleason's story is like something out of a movie, but it all happened in real life. He was a star athlete who played in the NFL, which is already a pretty impressive feat in itself, but what he did after facing one of the toughest challenges ever is even more incredible.

Steve was diagnosed with ALS, a very serious illness, but he didn't let that stop him at all. Instead, he decided to use his situation to help others and make a big difference. This chapter is all about how Steve keeps finding the beauty in every day and inspires everyone around him to do the same. Let's find out how Steve turned his challenge into a mission to help others and show the world how to fight and never give up on their dreams!

STEVE'S STORY

Starting life in Spokane, Washington, Steve Gleason was a kid full of energy and passion for sports. He played football, baseball, and basketball in high school, showing everyone his incredible talent and dedication.

In baseball, Steve broke the league record for home runs during his senior year. After graduating from high school, he went off to Washington State University, lighting up both the football field and the baseball diamond with his skills!

After college, Steve was eager to get into the NFL. Although he wasn't picked in the draft, he didn't give up. He started off with the Indianapolis Colts and then moved on to the New Orleans Saints, where he made a big splash on special teams. Steve is most famous for a single play—a blocked punt in a game that marked the New Orleans Superdome's reopening after Hurricane Katrina. This moment wasn't just a win for the team; it symbolized hope and rebirth for the entire city of New Orleans.

Life threw a tough challenge at Steve in 2011 when he was diagnosed with ALS, a severe illness that affects muscle control. Despite this, Steve's spirit remained unbroken. He used technology to keep speaking even after losing his voice and started Team Gleason, a group dedicated to helping others with ALS.

Steve didn't just raise awareness for the disease; he pushed for new laws to help patients get the communication tools they need. Team Gleason is dedicated to providing these advanced technological aids to people diagnosed with ALS and other similar diseases. Team Gleason's mission is to help provide individuals with the necessary tools to continue living productive and meaningful lives and also raise awareness.

Steve's efforts with his foundation led the U.S. Congress to draft the Steve Gleason Act. For all his incredible work, Steve was awarded the Congressional Gold Medal in 2020, one of the highest honors a civilian can receive in the United States.

Today, Steve continues to inspire people all over the world. His story teaches us about the strength of the human spirit and the power of hope. He shows us that even in the face of tough challenges, you can still make a difference in the world!

STEVE GLEASON FUN FACTS

- Gleason's blocked punt in 2006 has been immortalized with a statue titled "Rebirth" that was built outside the Superdome, the home of the New Orleans Saints.
- Steve's battle with ALS and his efforts to improve the lives of others with the disease was chronicled in the documentary *Gleason*.
- Steve challenged big tech companies to create new solutions for ALS patients, leading to the development of eye-tracking technology that lets people use computers and wheelchairs just by moving their eyes.

THINGS TO THINK ABOUT

- How can Steve's story inspire us to face challenges with courage and determination?
- What things do you want to raise awareness for? What are the things that affect you?
- What can we learn from the fact that Steve may have had to stop playing football, but didn't stop working as hard as he did even when he was physically unable to do a lot?

UP NEXT

As we close the chapter on Steve Gleason's inspiring journey of ALS advocacy, we can see how one individual's courage can ignite hope and drive change, even when we face some pretty steep personal challenges. Gleason's legacy teaches us that with determination and a desire to help others, we can make a significant impact, regardless of the obstacles we face.

Turning the page of Steve's story, we now turn our attention to another incredible narrative of persistence and triumph in the world of football. Kurt Warner's journey from an undrafted free agent to becoming an NFL MVP and Super Bowl champion is a powerful reminder that no dream is too big and that belief in oneself, combined with hard work and faith, can lead to some pretty big achievements. As you'll find out, Warner's story isn't just about football; it's about never giving up!

Chapter 15

KURT WARNER

The greatest impact you can have on people is never what you say but how you live... You set the standard with your actions. The words can come after.

–KURT WARNER

In the world of sports, sometimes the most inspiring stories aren't just about winning games or scoring touchdowns—they're about the journey it takes to get there. Kurt Warner's story is one of those. Imagine being a young person with big dreams; probably not too hard right, because I bet you already are!

Imagine finding yourself working late nights stocking shelves at a grocery store, far from the bright lights of NFL stadiums, while your dreams seem so far away. It sounds tough, right? But for many aspiring sports stars, this is just how life ends up. Only a very small percentage of the top players have what it takes to go pro.

But Kurt Warner's story, with his incredible belief in himself and relentless determination, shows us all how any moment could be the start of something amazing. He lived by the idea that actions speak louder than words, setting an example that anything is possible when you keep faith and never give up on your dreams.

KURT'S STORY

Born in the city of Burlington, Iowa, Kurt Warner's path from just a regular kid to NFL stardom is nothing short of amazing. The ultimate underdog story, Kurt spent his early years working hard, and only later got a big payoff, a pattern that would continue throughout his football career.

After graduating from high school, the next stop for Kurt was the University of Northern Iowa. He had to wait all the way until he reached senior year to even catch a break on the field. Only then did his coach finally decide to put him in as the starting quarterback. This late arrival to the spotlight didn't discourage Kurt; instead, it fueled his tenacity and showcased the early signs of the perseverance that would come to define his career.

After college, the NFL didn't immediately welcome Kurt with open arms. Instead, he joined the Arena Football League, playing for the Iowa Barnstormers. There, Kurt starred brilliantly, setting the stage for eventual entry into the NFL, but first, he would have a stopover in Europe with the NFL's overseas division.

Warner flew off to Amsterdam to play with the Admirals. Once he started playing in that league, he started to do really well, leading the European league in passing yards and touchdowns, and catching the attention of the NFL scouts back home in America. They started to wonder why they sent him off to Europe in the first place, as his skills were really picking up. Kurt was showing the world his untapped potential and readiness for bigger stages.

Kurt Warner's major NFL breakthrough came in a totally unexpected way. After playing in the European league, he returned to America to play with the St. Louis Rams. Kurt spent a lot of time on the bench until he got the opportunity of a lifetime. Starting quarterback Trent Green got injured, and the coaches decided to put Kurt in to sub for him. Kurt was suddenly in the limelight. He seized this opportunity spectacularly, going from being an unknown player to a leader of the "Greatest Show on Turf," a nickname Rams fans gave the revamped killer offensive line under Kurt.

Under Warner's leadership, the Rams clinched a Super Bowl win for the 1999 season. During the Rams' win, Kurt didn't just earn MVP honors—he also launched one of the most explosive offenses in NFL history as the "Greatest Show on Turf" continued on into the next seasons. Kurt's cabinet was beginning to fill up with all kinds of different awards and honors, including an additional MVP award in 2001.

Things calmed down a bit for Kurt in the next few seasons, but he still remained a solid player. In 2005, he got signed to the Arizona Cardinals. The Cardinals were a team more famous for their losses than their wins. In fact, they had never even made it to the Super Bowl. Under Kurt's leadership, that was about to change. He managed to take them to the Super Bowl for the 2008 season, which was a huge milestone in Cardinals franchise history, even though they ended up losing to the Pittsburgh Steelers.

As a QB, Kurt's amazing abilities didn't just lie in the fact that he could rally his teams together; he also boasted amazing stats for completions and passing yards, which landed him a place in the Pro Football Hall of Fame. Even after hanging up his cleats, Kurt has continued to inspire others through his involvement in charity efforts, most notably with his First Things First Foundation. His life beyond football remains a source of motivation for many, proving that his legacy stretches far beyond the gridiron.

KURT WARNER FUN FACTS

- Kurt was the first player to have thrown over 400 yards in a Super Bowl game, a feat matched only by Tom Brady (*Most 400 Yard Passing Games in Super Bowl*, n.d.).
- Kurt holds Super Bowl records for most passing yards in a game and career.
- Kurt Warner got a late start in football. By the time he joined the Rams, he was already 28 years old!
- Warner's story of perseverance and success was so compelling, it was adapted into a movie called *American Underdog*.

THINGS TO THINK ABOUT

- Kurt's journey from a humble grocery store clerk to an NFL superstar teaches us that all big dreams start with small, often humble beginnings. What are some small steps you can take today toward a big dream you have?
- Kurt didn't become a starting quarterback in college until his senior year and didn't start in the NFL until he was 28. How can you apply the same persistence to challenges in your life, like a subject in school that's tough for you?
- Warner's setbacks, like not making the NFL initially and then being demoted to a backup, set the stage for his future successes. What's one example of a setback you've faced that might be setting you up for something great in the future?

UP NEXT

As we leave behind the inspiring underdog story of Kurt Warner, whose journey from a grocery store to NFL greatness captivates and motivates, we turn our focus to another towering figure in football: Deion Sanders!

Deion wasn't just known for his electrifying athleticism, but also for his vibrant personality. From his triumphs to the influential presence he had in sports media and coaching, Deion Sanders' pro football career continues to leave an enduring impact on the world of sports. As we explore his story, we'll uncover how the man they called "Prime Time" used his flair, speed, and charisma to transform every field he stepped onto.

Chapter 16

DEION SANDERS

If you look good, you feel good. If you feel good, you play well. If you play well, they pay well.

–DEION SANDERS

Deion Sanders, famously known as "Prime Time," truly embodies his nickname by highlighting the electrifying presence he had on and off the field. When he was just a little kid, he used his confidence and flair to rise above a challenging family environment and focus his energy on his athletic talent.

Deion's journey from a multi-talented college athlete to a dual-sport professional player in both the NFL and Major League Baseball isn't just a story of sports success but of an unyielding belief in one's own abilities and the sheer will to succeed. This chapter will explore how Deion Sanders harnessed his unique talents to achieve greatness in sports and beyond, inspiring us all to embrace our individuality and pursue excellence in every arena of life.

DEION'S STORY

Deion Sanders was born in Fort Myers, Florida. Deion's parents split up when he was just a little kid, which was tough on him.

His dad had some tough times with his health and other problems. Deion didn't let these hard times keep him down, though. He found something he loved early on—sports!

By age eight, Deion was already playing organized baseball and football. He wasn't just good at one sport; he was terrific at several. In high school, he played football, basketball, and baseball, and he was one of the best in all of them. He could throw a football, hit a baseball, and shoot hoops like a star.

One night after a basketball game where he scored 30 points, a friend called him "Prime Time." That nickname stuck because Deion was always at his best when everyone was watching. It was like he was made for the big moments, always ready to show how great he could be, no matter the game or the challenge.

By the time Deion got to high school, he was playing football, basketball, and baseball. His exceptional athleticism didn't go unnoticed—as he managed to get state honors! This early success set him up for what would be a great college career, and many expected that he would also have a chance at the pros in at least one of the sports he played.

Attending Florida State University, Sanders didn't just play football; he was a standout in baseball and also participated in track and field. His college career was marked by All-American honors in football and numerous records in punt returns, displaying his versatility and setting a bunch of school records that still stand today.

Drafted into the NFL fifth overall by the Atlanta Falcons in 1989, Deion made an immediate impact by returning a punt for a touchdown in his very first game. This debut was just a hint of the kinds of dynamic and game-changing performances that he'd become known for.

The NFL wasn't the only professional sports league where Deion was making big moves, as he was still serious about baseball. He decided that he could balance his professional careers in both the NFL and Major League Baseball, and he went on to play for MLB teams including the Yankees, the Braves, the Reds, and finally, the San Francisco Giants (my home team!). His ability to play well in two major sports leagues simultaneously made him a rare and celebrated figure in sports history.

Deion was not just a flamboyant personality but also one of the most skilled cornerbacks in NFL history. His defensive play was characterized by high-speed interceptions and minimal opposing completions, earning him a reputation as a "shutdown" cornerback.

Over his career, Deion had two Super Bowl wins and went to the Pro Bowl eight times. In 1994, the NFL named him the AP Defensive Player of the Year.

When Deion decided to retire from football, he was inducted into the Pro Football Hall in addition to the College Football Hall of Fame, affirming his status as one of the greatest football players in the history of sports. Sanders transitioned to a coaching role and had a chance to impact young athletes' lives, first at Jackson State University, then at the University of Colorado.

After retiring from playing, Deion turned to coaching, where he has continued to make an impact on the game. Starting at Jackson State University and moving to the University of Colorado, Boulder, Sanders has used his platform to bring attention and resources to programs, making college football even more "Prime Time."

Deion's contributions extend beyond the playing field. He has been involved in youth sports programs and various community service efforts, using his platform to influence and improve the lives of young athletes across the country.

DEION SANDERS FUN FACTS

- While there have been other football players who also played professional baseball, Deion is the only one of them to have played in both a Super Bowl championship and an MLB World Series.
- After retiring from professional sports, Deion didn't disappear from the public eye; he became a beloved sports analyst and commentator, sharing his insights and charismatic personality on the NFL Network.
- Despite his busy sports career, Deion Sanders also released a rap album under his moniker, "Prime Time," in 1994.
- Deion was also known for being a very sharp dresser during the peak of his fame, his fashion choices both on and off the field making him a style icon in the sports world.
- Deion had a bunch of memorable catchphrases, including "Must be the money."

THINGS TO THINK ABOUT

- How did Deion's upbringing influence his career path and personality on and off the field?
- What can you learn from Deion's ability to play both professional football and baseball at the same time?
- How does Deion's post-retirement career as a coach and mentor reflect his ongoing commitment to sports and community?

UP NEXT

As we turn the page on Deion Sanders, whose impressive careers in both football and baseball, coupled with his unforgettable "Prime Time" persona, have deeply influenced the world of sports, our story now shifts to another iconic football figure.

Next, we'll be learning about Roger Staubach, a man whose skills on the football field and exemplary leadership have made him a legendary quarterback and one of the most fondly looked-upon figures in football history.

Chapter 17

ROGER STAUBACH

Confidence doesn't come out of nowhere. It's a result of something... hours and days and weeks and years of constant work and dedication.
—ROGER STAUBACH

Roger Staubach's path to NFL greatness, from a diligent Boy Scout to a celebrated naval officer and eventually a legendary NFL quarterback, shows us the true meaning of a life led by example. From his tour of duty in Vietnam to his subsequent rise as one of the most iconic quarterbacks in NFL history with the Dallas Cowboys, Roger tackled every undertaking with dedication and passion.

Known for his last-minute heroics and strategic playmaking, Roger helped make the Cowboys "America's Team." As a nation watched, jaws dropped as he made countless players that snatched victory from the jaws of defeat. As we learn Roger's story, we'll uncover how his early commitment to service shaped his character and leadership, both on the football field and beyond, into a successful business career. Roger's story teaches us valuable lessons about the power of perseverance, excellence, and the enduring impact of leading a disciplined life.

ROGER'S STORY

Roger Staubach was born in Cincinnati, Ohio. From a very young age, he showed a keen interest in outdoor activities, including sports. Aside from playing sports and games outside with his friends, he was also a Boy Scout. Being involved in the Scouts helped him develop solid leadership skills.

During high school, Roger began to take sports more seriously. By the time he graduated from high school, the stage had already been set for a stellar athletic career to come. The next stop for Roger would be the U.S. Naval Academy, where he'd be able to play football and serve his country.

Roger did great on the Navy team, where as QB, he rallied the team together and led them to victory while he set new records. In 1963, he was awarded the prestigious Heisman Trophy, recognizing him as the top collegiate football player in the entire country!

After graduating in 1965, Staubach honored his commitment to the Navy and served the country in Vietnam. His time in the military didn't just show his commitment to service—it also helped strengthen his leadership abilities, qualities that he would bring back to his professional sports career once he was able to get back to civilian life.

Once Roger had finished his military service, it was time to start thinking about the next step. Staubach's military discharge allowed him to join the Dallas Cowboys, a team that had drafted him back in 1964 as a future prospect. The transition was seamless due to his disciplined approach and leadership skills honed in the Navy. Now it would be time for Roger to apply his strategic thinking and physical agility on the football field instead of the battlefield.

Once with the Cowboys, Roger quickly became one of the top players in the league. His career in Dallas spanned a decade, during which he led the team to numerous playoff appearances and helped the Cowboys cement their reputation as "America's Team."

Staubach's leadership on the field was instrumental in leading the Dallas Cowboys to two Super Bowl victories, earning MVP honors in Super Bowl VI. His ability to perform under pressure earned him the nickname "Captain Comeback," due to his numerous fourth-quarter heroics.

Known for the agility he showed on the field, Roger was one of the first quarterbacks to use scrambling as an effective strategy, revolutionizing the role of the quarterback. His accurate passing and ability to avoid getting sacked made him a really tough opponent, changing the way other QBs played the position.

Roger retired from professional football in 1979 and was inducted into the Pro Football Hall of Fame in 1985. After football, Staubach found success in the world of real estate, building a highly successful business. His business skills followed his sportsmanship, and he applied the same integrity, commitment, and leadership that he learned on the field to all his other pursuits.

In 2018, Roger was awarded the Presidential Medal of Freedom, highlighting his contributions both on and off the field, including his charitable efforts and commitment to community service.

Roger Staubach's legacy in professional football goes way beyond his stats and his epic in-game performances. His life story shows us the importance of leadership skills, perseverance, and dedication. As a sports icon, veteran, businessman, and philanthropist, Roger's story continues to inspire and influence young athletes just like you!

ROGER STAUBACH FUN FACTS

- Roger is the only NFL player to have had a late start after serving in the military and still achieve such an illustrious career. He was already 27 by the time he joined the NFL.
- Roger is color-blind, which may have made it harder to see the ball on the field.
- Roger was known for his accurate arm with nimble footwork, which revolutionized quarterback play in the NFL.

THINGS TO THINK ABOUT

- How do you think Roger's service in the Navy helped shape his character and help him develop his leadership style on the football field?
- What lessons can you learn from Roger's perseverance in balancing his commitment to the Navy and his football career?
- How does Roger's post-football success in business inspire you? Do you want to have multiple career paths, or just play sports and not be interested in anything else?

UP NEXT

As we wrap up our exploration of Roger Staubach's storied career, from his disciplined beginnings at the Naval Academy through his triumphs in the NFL and successful ventures in business, we witness a life marked by unwavering leadership, commitment, and an ability to adapt across multiple arenas.

Roger's story sure gives us some deep lessons in perseverance and dedication. Now, it's time to look at another exceptional athlete whose career is equally inspiring. Larry Fitzgerald, remembered not just for his on-field achievements but also for his community involvement and leadership, gives us another powerful example of how dedication and belief in oneself can lead to great success both on and off the field.

Chapter 18

LARRY FITZGERALD

You can never let anything distract you from your main objective. My only goal is to be great. That's all I want. That's all I ever aspire to be. Greatness is something nobody can ever take away from you, no matter what happens. So I put all my energy and focus into my craft.

–LARRY FITZGERALD

In professional football, true greatness isn't something that can be measured by statistics or the ability to dazzle on the field. Real greatness comes from having integrity, dedication, and showing a real commitment to positively impacting the world. Larry Fitzgerald, one of the most highly regarded NFL players to ever hit the field, embodied these qualities and more.

Larry's path to football greatness wasn't just about his athleticism—it was one of deep personal commitment to excellence and service. His career, decorated with awe-inspiring records and characterized by unwavering sportsmanship, stands as a shining example of the game played well both on and off the field. Let's learn Larry's story!

LARRY'S STORY

Larry Fitzgerald's story started in Minneapolis, Minnesota, where he was born into a family with a strong love for sports. This environment helped encourage Larry and allowed his love for football and other sports to thrive from a very young age. His childhood was spent in the playgrounds and fields around his neighborhood, where he first learned to throw and catch a ball, setting him up for future success.

By the time he was ready to go off to high school, he was ready to start taking things more seriously. He found a spot on the team at a private Catholic school in Minnesota called Academy of Holy Angels. Once he was there and joined the team, Larry quickly made a name for himself in the athletics department.

Larry didn't just go there to play football; he also played basketball and was a valued member of the track team. Larry shone brightest on the football field though. His coach saw that he had multiple talents on the field and tried him out in a few different positions, but it soon became clear to all that Larry's talents were most apparent when he was playing wide receiver. His skills on the gridiron made him a local star, and he soon got a lot of attention from local college scouts.

Larry's football journey continued on at the University of Pittsburgh, where he further developed his skills. Despite facing challenges that made him have to do an extra year of school at Valley Forge Military Academy to meet the NCAA's academic eligibility requirements, Larry's college career was nothing short of amazing!

By his sophomore year, Larry wasn't just only a finalist for the Heisman Trophy—a rare feat for a wide receiver—but also a unanimous All-American. During college, he set numerous records and earned praise from cheering fans as he showed his incredible work ethic and talent on the field. Now it was time for Larry to start thinking about a bright future in the NFL.

In 2004, Larry's pro football dreams came true when he was drafted third overall by the Arizona Cardinals. His impact was immediate, and he quickly became one of the league's top receivers. Over his 17 seasons in the NFL, Larry was known for his reliability, great sportsmanship, and consistent performance, gaining a total of 11 Pro Bowl selections. His off-field endeavors, particularly his extensive charity work, earned him the prestigious Walter Payton NFL Man of the Year Award in 2016.

Larry Fitzgerald's influence extends beyond the football field. Known for his charity work, he has been involved in numerous charitable efforts, notably through the Larry Fitzgerald First Down Fund. His leadership qualities and ability to work effectively as part of a team have not only made him a role model for young athletes but also exemplify the importance of humility and teamwork in achieving great success.

Today, Larry is an avid traveler and photographer. He's explored countries across multiple continents, using his travels to learn about diverse cultures to drive the charity work that the First Down Fund does. On trips to Africa, Larry has visited schools and rural villages, using these visits to both provide support and raise awareness about the needs of underprivileged communities all around the world.

Larry often shares his travel experiences and the perspectives gained through his photography, reflecting a deep appreciation for the world's diverse cultures and peoples. His photography captures stunning landscapes and moments and also tells stories of places and people all over the world, highlighting their beauty and struggles alike.

LARRY FITZGERALD FUN FACTS

- Larry has a degree in communications, and he has always spoken about the importance of education throughout his career.
- Aside from having won the NFL's Walter Payton Man of the Year Award, Larry was known for his excellent sportsmanship; that's why he was also recognized with the Art Rooney Sportsmanship Award.
- Larry rarely missed out on any games due to injuries, showing his durability and ability to recover quickly and give it his all.

THINGS TO THINK ABOUT

- How does Larry's dedication to getting a good education inspire you in your own goals at school?
- What can you learn from Larry's approach to teamwork and leadership in both sports and community service?
- How does Larry having won a sportsmanship award show us that it's not just about all our skills, but about our attitude and approach to the game too?

UP NEXT

As we continue to reflect on Larry Fitzgerald's inspiring journey, marked by his great sportsmanship and charitable heart, it's now time to turn to the story of Russell Wilson. Like Fitzgerald, Wilson exemplifies talent and leadership on the field with a rock-solid commitment to his community and personal integrity.

Let's delve into how Wilson's career and off-field endeavors continue to inspire and influence those around him, paving the way for a legacy that stretches way beyond the boundaries of the football field.

Chapter 19

RUSSELL WILSON

*Always persevere, always have a great perspective,
and always have great purpose in your life.*

–RUSSELL WILSON

In the tough, competitive environment of the NFL, where physical strength too often overshadows other qualities, Russell Wilson stands out from other players, and it's not just for the exceptional skills he showed on the field as a quarterback, but for his great leadership skills and determined spirit.

Russel's path from multi-talented high school athlete to Super Bowl champion, is a story about much more than sports excellence. It's a story filled with perseverance, community action, and an indomitable belief that he could succeed against all odds.

Let's find out exactly how Russel's early influences shaped him into the NFL leader he is today and look at the impact he's had both as one of today's greatest quarterbacks and a committed do-gooder off the field.

RUSSELL'S STORY

Russell was born in Cincinnati, Ohio, but his family ended up moving to Richmond, Virginia, where he grew up. It was there that his passion for football really started to take root. Raised in a family that was supportive of his athletic ambitions, Russell's father, a former NFL prospect turned lawyer, played an important role in encouraging Russel to play sports, and gave him a strong work ethic that he'd hold onto his whole life.

At the Collegiate School in Richmond, Russell showed early signs of his versatile athletic ability. He didn't just excel at football; he was also a great baseball player and was prolific on the basketball court. Most importantly, from an early age, he began showing the strong leadership qualities that would come to define his career.

By the time he was ready for college, Russell was looking for a school where he could really dig his cleats into the dirt. He found that at North Carolina State University, where he demonstrated remarkable skills that earned him all-ACC honors as a freshman. Russell was still taking baseball pretty seriously, too, though.

Russell's continued interest in both sports led him to consider transferring to another school that had a good baseball team. That's how, eventually, he ended up transferring to the University of Wisconsin, where he did well in both baseball and football. Though he still loved both sports, he was emerging quickly as a rising football star. He was soon setting new records, including the one for a single-season FBS record for passing efficiency.

Standing at 5' 11'", Russell wasn't short by any means, but some thought that he wasn't big enough to play with the pros. Russell proved the doubters wrong, however; his skills on the field were recognized by everyone who saw him play. They could see that he was a star, and he was about to prove it with his pro football debut.

Russell was the third-round draft pick for the Seattle Seahawks in 2012—his selection soon proved to be a game-changer for the team. By his second season with the Seahawks, Russell had already left an indelible mark on the NFL, leading the team to victory in the Super Bowl for the 2013 season, firming up his status among the league's elite quarterbacks.

Throughout his career, Russell has set numerous records, including the most wins by a quarterback in his first nine seasons (*Most Wins by a QB in Their First 9 Seasons*, n.d.). Known for his relentless work ethic, Russell spends countless hours studying game film and practicing, continuously striving to improve his performance. Over the years, Russell's consistency and skills on the field have earned him multiple Pro Bowl selections, building him a reputation as one of the best quarterbacks in the whole league.

Off the field, Russell is well known for all kinds of charitable work he does, especially his regular visits to the Seattle Children's Hospital and his involvement with the Why Not You Foundation, which focuses on education, children's health, and helping kids from poor backgrounds.

One of the impacts of the Why Not You Foundation is its scholarship program, which gives scholarships to student leaders who want to make a big difference in the world. By investing in these young students, Russell aims to cultivate a generation that, like him, believes in achieving both personal and community-wide goals.

Russell's leadership extends into his interactions with his teammates and the broader Seattle community, where he's considered a local legend. Known for his positive demeanor and relentless work ethic, he has been a solid leader for the Seahawks, often seen rallying his team with motivational words and leading by example. His approach to leadership is inclusive and supportive, encouraging an environment on the field and in the locker room, where his teammates feel valued and motivated to excel.

Russell's leadership extends beyond personal achievements, inspiring his teammates with his commitment and positive attitude, both on and off the field. He still loves baseball too, and was even drafted by the Colorado Rockies, and later by the Yankees, who still hold Russell's pro baseball rights in case he ever decides to get back into it.

RUSSELL WILSON FUN FACTS

- Russell is considered an outstanding QB because of his mobility and "pocket presence."
- He's married to a pop star, the musical artist Ciara! Russell loves all different kinds of music, including her music, of course.
- Russell was a big Seahawks fan before he even got drafted, making the deal all the sweeter!
- Russell is a mentor for lots of young athletes like you, helping them develop skills and pursue careers in sports.

THINGS TO THINK ABOUT

- How does Russell's willingness to help kids like you get good at sports inspire you to help others?
- What lessons can you learn from Russell's ability to overcome adversity and prove his doubters wrong?
- In what ways do Russell's strong work ethic and dedication to constant improvement by watching footage of his plays over and over again inspire you to get better at the things you care about?

UP NEXT

As we turn the page on Russell Wilson, you've now seen his inspiring journey to sports greatness up close. Russell is truly one of the NFL's best QBs, but more importantly, he's a guy whose remarkable talents on the football field are matched only by his unwavering commitment to improving his own game, leadership, and helping others.

Russell's story shows us how determination, community engagement, and a passion for excellence can help us achieve personal triumphs and make a difference in the lives of others. With these themes in mind, it's now time to take a look at another top figure in football. Up next, we'll be learning the story of Tom Dempsey, a player whose own unique challenges and triumphs brought him to prominence in America's great game.

Chapter 20

TOM DEMPSEY

To be a good field goal kicker you have to ignore all the external factors. Focus solely on that spot on the ground.

–TOM DEMPSEY

Imagine that you had the ability to kick a football further than anyone else, even when everyone watching says there's no way you can possibly do it, just because of the way you were born. That's the incredible story of Tom Dempsey summed up. He was a football player who dreamed big and then made his dreams come true despite all the challenges he faced.

You see, Tom was born with a bunch of missing toes and fingers. Instead of giving up on sports though, he turned the unique differences he was born with into a golden opportunity, landing in the pros. Wearing a special shoe designed to fit him, he could kick field goal after field goal, and nobody could stop him!

As it turned out, Tom's supposed "handicap" gave him amazing power and accuracy with kicking the ball, allowing him to make history by kicking one of the longest field goals ever recorded in NFL history. Let's learn Tom's story, and see how his courage, creativity, and will to never give up on his dreams brought him to the top.

TOM'S STORY

Tom Dempsey was born in Milwaukee, Wisconsin into a world that might have seen him as being limited as far as the choices he'd be able to make in life. His right foot didn't have any toes at all, and he also had no fingers on his right hand. Due to him being different from other kids, Tom faced challenges that most of us could never imagine. When he was very young, his family moved to San Diego, California, and that was where he grew up.

In sunny southern California, Tom loved to play outside with other kids, and rather than be overprotective of him due to his physical differences, his parents decided to just let Tom play like any other kid. From a young age, he was especially interested in playing football, never letting his physical differences hold him back from his favorite game.

Tom's foray into football presented him with a unique challenge though: kicking. Though being able to punt the ball isn't the main focus of most gameplay, it's still an important skill to develop. It was especially important for Tom because everyone told him he could never do it.

Now it was up to Tom to prove them all wrong. Tom's dad was especially supportive of him, continually telling him that he could do anything he set his heart to. He kept on believing in himself and decided that he was going to play football no matter what because it was what he loved to do. Tom also was really into baseball at the time, and became an all-star.

Tom went off to high school and was eager to get on the football team. He also continued to play baseball, wrestled, and did shotput in track and field. To be able to play on the team as a lineman, Tom's dad had a custom shoe made for him that had a big, flat toe area which turned his perceived disadvantage into a powerful tool on the field.

It was like kicking the ball with a giant swinging hammer! Spectators watched in awe as Tom's kicks would fly high up into the sky with amazing force, and then would sail between the goal posts with impressive accuracy.

Tom's football career continued at Palomar College, where his skills were honed further. His time playing college football was a testament to his relentless spirit and determination, setting the stage for an unexpected professional career that would inspire millions.

Undrafted and highly underestimated by almost everyone, Tom still had what it took to enter the NFL as a dedicated kicker, joining the New Orleans Saints. His powerful kicks soon made waves, proving that skill and determination can outshine doubt. Tom quickly became known for his presence on the field and his inspiring story of overcoming the odds.

The highlight of Tom Dempsey's NFL career came on November 8, 1970. In a game against the Detroit Lions, Tom set a record with a stunning 63-yard field goal. This historic kick didn't just clinch the game—it stood as an NFL record for 43 years all the way until 2013 (Donahue, 2023b)! It was a kick that defied the odds and made Tom recognized as a true football legend for decades to come.

Tom's record-breaking performance was more than just a personal victory; it was a demonstration that limitations could be overcome with creativity and courage. His achievement inspired both players and fans, showing that barriers are meant to be broken.

Tom's career didn't stop with the Saints. He played for several other NFL teams, including the Philadelphia Eagles, Los Angeles Rams, Houston Oilers, and Buffalo Bills. Each phase of his career added chapters to his legacy as a player who could always be counted on for his strong kicking ability.

After retiring from professional football, Tom Dempsey's life continued to be a source of inspiration. His famous 63-yard kick remained a highlight of NFL history, encouraging future generations of kickers to push the limits of what is possible on the football field.

Choosing to move back to New Orleans after his retirement, Tom was celebrated as a local hero. He continued to inspire people with his story, proving that heroes come in many forms and often, from unexpected places.

Later in life, Tom began to experience some tough health challenges. He got dementia, which means he started losing his memory. This meant that he could no longer remember all the great kicks he had or the records he set. Despite Tom's inability to remember, those around him did, and he was still a hero to them!

When Tom passed away in 2020, the NFL and sports fans across the country all paid tribute to his remarkable career and the obstacles he overcame, celebrating a life that went beyond the game of football, giving those with physical differences hope for a bright future despite their supposed handicaps or disabilities.

TOM DEMPSEY FUN FACTS

- Tom was a really big guy, which allowed him to really throw his weight into his kicks. He weighed up to 300 lbs. during his career (Didinger, 2020).
- Some thought that Tom's special shoe gave him an unfair advantage, and there were even rumors going around that the special shoe might have weights in it to make his kicks more powerful. This was shown to be untrue—Tom was really just that strong!
- To further debunk the theory that he had an unfair advantage, ESPN Sport Science did a study on Tom's custom-made kicking shoe and found that it actually made it harder for Tom to kick

versus someone wearing a regular shoe (*Was Tom Dempsey's Disability Actually an Advantage?*, 2022).

- By the time Tom retired from the NFL, he had made 159 field goals on 258 attempts, an impressive 61.6% (Donahue, 2023b).

- In 1972, playing with the Philadelphia Eagles, Tom kicked six field goals in a single game against the Houston Oilers, a record that still holds today (Didinger, 2020). Amazingly, the Eagles won the game, with all their points being scored by Tom's field goals!

THINGS TO THINK ABOUT

- Tom never let his physical condition limit his dreams. What is something you find difficult, and how can you use determination to improve or succeed in it?

- Tom had a lot of encouragement from his dad and his coaches, which helped him achieve his goals. Who are the people who support you in your life, and how do they help you achieve your goals?

- Dempsey was more than just a kicker; he saw himself as a full football player. Why do you think it's important to look beyond labels and see all aspects of a person's abilities?

UP NEXT

As we close the chapter on Tom Dempsey, it's time to gear up for yet another football tale. J.J. Watt was a player whose journey wasn't just about athletic skill but was also about making a big impact in his community.

From electrifying plays on the football field to heartfelt charity work off the field, Watt's story shows us the power of hard work and how having a big heart is even more important than being good at sports. Join us as we discover how this NFL superstar has turned obstacles into opportunities for greatness and generosity.

Chapter 21

J.J. WATT

If you want to be remembered as great, if you want to be a legend, you have to go out there every single day and do stuff.

–J.J. WATT

Imagine waking up every day with a mission; a mission not just to be good, but to be great. Not just to play hard, but to make a real difference in the world. That's the story of J.J. Watt, a towering figure on the football field who uses his strength not just to tackle linemen, but to lift up entire communities when they are down.

Born in a small town in Wisconsin, J.J. Watt started out like most of us do, with big dreams and skinned knees. But as we'll see, it wasn't just his talent in sports that made him a star; it was his heart.

From smashing records on the field to raising millions for people in need, J.J.'s journey to NFL success and his post-career humanitarian work show us that being a legend isn't just about what you do in the spotlight—it's about how you help others shine too.

Let's take a look at J.J.'s story, a tale of football success where every sack and every dollar raised tells a story of determination, compassion, and the unstoppable power of dreaming big.

J.J.'S STORY

Growing up in Wisconsin, young J.J. Watt discovered his passion for sports. With dreams as big as his smile, J.J. didn't just play football—he also was involved in hockey, and track and field throughout his school years. Even as a kid, J.J. had the heart of a champion, but it was his relentless drive and love for competition that shaped his early interest in sports.

In high school, J.J. continued to focus on sports while working really hard at his studies too. This allowed him to get into Central Michigan, where he'd be able to pursue football along with his academic goals. J.J. joined the team as a tight end, but he transferred to another school: the University of Wisconsin-Madison. Once he was at his new college, J.J.'s coaches put him on defense. He believed that he'd truly found his calling. It felt like the position he was meant to play!

J.J.'s standout performance as a defenseman with the University of Wisconsin-Madison's Badgers began to gain national attention, setting the stage for a bright future in the NFL. In 2011, the Houston Texans, seeing J.J.'s great potential in pro football, selected him as the 11th overall pick in the draft. This was just the beginning of what would become a legendary professional career.

It didn't take long for J.J. to make a name for himself in the NFL. Known for his fierce ability to sack quarterbacks and disrupt offenses, he quickly became one of the league's most dominant defensive players. J.J.'s playing rippled throughout the entire league, and he ended up getting named the NFL Defensive Player of the Year multiple times. Each award he got was well deserved for the skill, determination, and leadership he showed on the field.

J.J. was truly a star, but it was his work off the field that would make him a true legend. As the creator of the J.J. Watt Foundation, he has focused on providing after-school opportunities for children, showing that his passion extends beyond football to empowering the next generation. But that's not all!

In 2017, J.J. demonstrated amazing leadership and compassion by raising over $37 million for Hurricane Harvey relief efforts in Houston (*Hurricane Harvey Relief Efforts*, n.d.). J.J.'s direct actions and fundraising efforts helped rebuild communities and restore hope to countless individuals and families. That same year, J.J. was honored with the Walter Payton NFL Man of the Year Award, honoring his excellence in both his athletic performance and his charitable efforts. This award highlighted how he embodies the spirit of community and perseverance.

Throughout his career, J.J. set multiple records, including being the first player in NFL history to record two seasons with more than 20 sacks (*Most Seasons with 20 or More Sacks by a Player*, n.d.). These achievements have given him a standing in NFL history right alongside all the other icons featured in this book.

Known for his leadership both on and off the field, J.J. has served as a captain, guiding younger players and setting a high standard for professionalism and dedication. His leadership extends beyond performance, encompassing his commitment to team and community.

Beyond his athletic and charity efforts, J.J. is known for his engaging personality and active presence on social media, where he loves talking to his fans. One of the greatest things about J.J. is that he approaches his fame with humility and a sense of responsibility, always wanting to make a positive impact on and off the field rather than just be famous for fame's sake.

In 2022, J.J. Watt announced his retirement from professional football, marking the end of an illustrious career. Despite the physical demands and injuries that came with over a decade in the NFL, J.J.'s love for the game never waned. His retirement was met with widespread admiration and gratitude from fans, teammates, and rivals alike, who celebrated his contributions on the field and the impact he's made.

As he stepped away from the gridiron for the last time, J.J. expressed a desire to spend more time with his family and to continue his charity work, ensuring that his legacy would extend far beyond his football achievements.

J.J.'s path to football greatness, from a sports-loving kid in Wisconsin to a renowned NFL star and all-around good guy, is a powerful reminder of how dedication, hard work, and a big heart can make all the difference in this world.

J.J.'s story isn't just about all the great plays he made, it's also about using one's talents and platform to bring about positive change. J.J. Watt continues to inspire both young athletes and the broader community, showing that success is not just about what you accomplish but also about how you use your achievements to help others.

J.J. WATT FUN FACTS

- J.J. was known for his grueling training routines and commitment to improving his skills.
- J.J. has made appearances on television shows and in movies, showing how his popularity with the public goes way beyond the football field.
- In 2012, J. J. Watt recorded a staggering 20.5 sacks in a single season, holding the record for the most sacks in a single season by a Texans player (Rolon, 2023).

THINGS TO THINK ABOUT

- How does J.J. Watt's commitment to community service inspire you to contribute to your community?
- J.J. is known for his incredible work ethic. Why do you think hard work is important, and how can you apply a strong work ethic in your own pursuits, whether in sports, school, or hobbies?
- J.J. Watt had many physical challenges and injuries throughout his career which led to his decision to retire. What are some obstacles you face in your own activities or life, and how can you apply J.J.'s perseverance to overcome them?

WRAPPING THINGS UP

As we still have the story of one of football's most remarkable figures J.J. Watt in our minds, we've again seen just how impactful dedication, hard work, and a commitment to helping others can have on the world. The tales we've explored in this book illuminate the powerful notion that success on the field is merely the beginning.

These athletes' contributions extend way beyond game-winning plays and record-breaking performances; they resonate in the lives they touch, the communities they uplift, and the lasting legacies they build. Let all these stories, J.J.'s included, inspire us not just to dream big but to act with purpose and kindness in all our endeavors.

YOUR TURN TO INSPIRE!

Just like every single one of the players you've read about, you can make your mark on the world. Let these stories be your inspiration… and take a moment now to inspire someone else.

Simply by sharing your honest opinion of this book and a little about what you found here, you'll show new readers where they can find a treasure trove of inspiration.

MAKE A LASTING IMPRESSION!

Thank you so much for your support. You've barely begun, and you're already making a difference!

Scan the QR code below

CONCLUSION

As we close the pages of this inspiring journey through the lives of football's most remarkable figures, we are left with a profound sense of admiration and motivation. In each chapter, we took a close look at the performance and records set by these legends, but we also looked deep into their personal lives, revealing the resilience, dedication, and altruism that define true greatness.

From the story of Tom Dempsey, who overcame physical challenges to set a long-standing NFL record, to J.J. Watt, whose off-the-field humanitarian efforts have shown us that the influence of a sports star can extend far beyond the stadium, this book has offered a glimpse into the myriad of challenges these athletes have faced and conquered.

From the media spotlight of Michael Strahan's second career in TV, to the strategic brilliance of Russell Wilson to the quiet strength of Tom Brady, each story we've looked at leaves us with enduring impressions of what it truly means to be great. The big takeaway from it all, if you ask me, is the idea that success on the field is just the beginning of a larger story—one that can inspire change and bring about a positive impact in the wider world.

Football's legendary players, both past and present, offer us a window into all the different personal and professional challenges they faced and the diverse ways they overcame them. Their stories aren't just about athletic performance, rather, they serve as timeless lessons of character, fortitude, and athletic, cultural, social, and community impact that continue to inspire beyond the realm of sports.

These stories are not just about football; they're also about the human spirit's capacity for perseverance and the constant pursuit of excellence regardless of the hurdles we face. They teach us that setbacks can be the stepping stones to greatness and that every day offers a new opportunity to make an impact.

As you reflect on the extraordinary lives of these athletes, consider how their stories resonate with your own experiences and aspirations. Think about the tenacity of Russell Wilson, who never allowed his initial undersized and underappreciated status deter him from becoming a Super Bowl champion and a revered leader.

Never forget Walter Payton's grace under pressure, Drew Brees' impact on his community, Jim Brown's activism, and John Madden's turning a big disappointment that kept him on the bench into a successful, long career as a coach and commentator.

These narratives also ask us to look deeper into the rich history of the game itself. Football, after all, is a sport that mirrors many of life's most valuable lessons—teamwork, discipline, and the relentless pursuit of goals—all played on the gridiron. Each story in this book serves as a starting point for your own exploration and discovery. Whether you are a sports enthusiast, a budding athlete, or someone passionate about history, there is much to learn from these iconic figures.

Moreover, let these stories inspire you to pursue your passions, whatever they may be. In the face of adversity, remember the resilience shown by these athletes. When faced with the opportunity to help others, think of the generosity and spirit of community that shines through their actions. And in moments of doubt, recall their dedication to improvement and mastery of their craft.

Take these lessons into your own lives; use them as fuel to overcome your challenges, to reach out to others, and to strive for excellence in every endeavor. Whether you're on the sports field, in the classroom, at home, or simply out playing with your friends, remember that your actions have the power to inspire and influence those around you.

Remember, each setback you face is a setup for a comeback. Keep smiling like Deion Sanders, and keep a positive cheerful attitude like Gronk always does. If you stick to acting like these pros, you'll be able to harness the true power of their stories and the lessons they share with us, helping you reach goals in your life, and maybe even inspire others along the way.

Finally, as we conclude this exploration of football's most incredible stories, I truly hope that you feel a renewed sense of motivation. Let the courage and integrity of these legends encourage you to make your own mark in the world, to be a leader in your community, and to use your talents to foster positive change.

I'd like to invite you or your parents to share your thoughts about this book. If these stories have inspired you, consider leaving a review to help others discover the motivational power of these incredible athletes' lives. Your feedback doesn't just help support all the sports research I do to bring you the stories of greats in all different sports, it also encourages others to explore these compelling stories. If you haven't read my baseball book yet, and are a fan of that sport, you should definitely check it out! I'm working on a basketball one too that should be in stores shortly!

In closing, remember that each one of us has the potential to achieve greatness. Like the football legends featured in this book, you have the unique opportunity to use your strengths to overcome obstacles, to excel, and to positively impact the world around you. Let their legacies inspire you to act, to dream, and to achieve with the same unyielding spirit of determination and generosity.

So, with that said, go forth with the wisdom and inspiration you've gained, and remember: The field is wide open, and the game is yours to win, both on and off the gridiron!

REFERENCES

Abdalazem, R. (2023, August 14). *What is Michael Oher's story? The real Michael who inspired "The Blind Side."* Diario AS. https://en.as.com/nfl/what-is-michael-ohers-story-the-real-michael-who-inspired-the-blind-side-n/

About JJ. (n.d.). Justin J. Watt Foundation. https://jjwfoundation.org/about-jj/

About Steve Gleason. (n.d.). Team Gleason. https://teamgleason.org/steve-story/

Allen, S. (2024, February 8). Super Bowl records come and go. Jerry Rice's endure. *Washington Post*. https://www.washingtonpost.com/sports/2024/02/08/jerry-rice-super-bowl-records/

Always persevere, always have a great perspective, and always have great purpose in your life. (n.d.). QuoteFancy. Retrieved April 14, 2024, from https://quotefancy.com/quote/1731342/Russell-Wilson-Always-persevere-always-have-a-great-perspective-and-always-have-great

Angeles, F. (2024, March 4). *25 surprising facts about John Madden*. Facts.net. https://facts.net/celebrity/25-surprising-facts-about-john-madden/

Apple, C. (2020, January 16). *The life and times of Steve Gleason and ALS*. The Spokesman Review. https://www.spokesman.com/stories/2020/jan/16/life-and-times-steve-gleason-and-als/

Ash, C. (2023, August 9). *48 facts about Russell Wilson*. Facts.net. https://facts.net/celebrity/48-facts-about-russell-wilson/

Athlete. scholar. soldier. leader. (2018). Pat Tillman Foundation. https://pattillmanfoundation.org/the-foundation/pats-story/

Augustyn, A. (2019). John Madden. In *Encyclopædia Britannica*. https://www.britannica.com/biography/John-Madden

Augustyn, A. (2024a, March 10). *Michael Strahan*. Encyclopaedia Britannica. https://www.britannica.com/biography/Michael-Strahan

Augustyn, A. (2024b, April 9). *Deion Sanders*. Encyclopedia Britannica. https://www.britannica.com/biography/Deion-Sanders

Battista, J. (2021, December 28). *John Madden's unparalleled impact on NFL influenced generations of football fans*. NFL.com. https://www.nfl.com/news/john-madden-s-unparalleled-impact-on-nfl-influenced-generations-of-football-fans

Bender, B. (2019, January 31). *Deion sanders: 21 amazing facts about prime time's two-way career*. The Sporting News. https://www.sportingnews.com/us/

nfl/news/deion-sanders-21-amazing-facts-about-prime-times-two-way-career/1ak1w6tck57i11e2vn5le7g5u3

Biography Editors, & McEvoy, C. (2021, May 27). *Michael Oher*. Biography. https://www.biography.com/athletes/michael-oher

Biography.com Editors. (2017, April 28). *Pat Tillman*. Biography. https://www.biography.com/athlete/pat-tillman

Biography.com Editors. (2023a, November 9). *Peyton Manning*. Biography. https://www.biography.com/athletes/peyton-manning

Biography.com Editors. (2023b, November 17). *Kurt Warner*. Biography. https://www.biography.com/athletes/a45875740/kurt-warner

Biography.com Editors, & Piccotti, T. (2021, April 9). *Jim Brown*. Biography. https://www.biography.com/athletes/jim-brown

Bitler, D. (2022, March 24). *Happy birthday, Peyton Manning; 10 facts about the sheriff.* FOX31 Denver. https://kdvr.com/sports/denver-broncos/happy-birthday-peyton-manning-10-facts-about-the-sheriff/

Brady, T. (n.d.). *Tom Brady quotes*. BrainyQuote. https://www.brainyquote.com/quotes/tom_brady_682465

Brees, D. (n.d.). *Drew Brees quotes*. BrainyQuote. https://www.brainyquote.com/quotes/drew_brees_1063872

Brown, J. (n.d.). *Jim Brown quotes*. BrainyQuote. https://www.brainyquote.com/quotes/jim_brown_803249

Bueno, G. (2023, October 7). *18 extraordinary facts about Michael Oher*. Facts.net. https://facts.net/celebrity/18-extraordinary-facts-about-michael-oher/

CardinalsFanGirl. (2017, October 6). *5 fun facts about Cardinals' Larry Fitzgerald Jr.* Fangirl Sports Network. https://fgsn.com/5-fun-facts-cardinals-larry-fitzgerald-jr/

Cardona, T. (2024, March 4). *9 extraordinary facts about Drew Brees*. Facts.net. https://facts.net/celebrity/9-extraordinary-facts-about-drew-brees/

Cash, M. (2023, February 1). *20 things you might not have known about Tom Brady*. Business Insider. https://www.businessinsider.com/facts-about-tom-brady-you-didnt-know-patriots-buccaneers-2023-2#12-he-is-ridiculously-competitive-12

CNN Editorial Research. (2023, May 24). *Jim Brown fast facts*. CNN. https://edition.cnn.com/2014/01/15/us/jim-brown-fast-facts/index.html

Cobos, S. (2024, March 2). *48 facts about Deion Sanders*. Facts.net. https://facts.net/celebrity/48-facts-about-deion-sanders/

College days: Jim Kelly. (n.d.). Pro Football Hall of Fame. Retrieved May 12, 2024, from https://www.profootballhof.com/news/2013/10/news-college-days-jim-kelly/

de la Rosa, P. (2022, June 30). *What happened to Larry Fitzgerald? (Story)*. Pro Football History. https://www.profootballhistory.com/larry-fitzgerald/

DeArdo , B. (2023, October 13). *Jerry Rice turns 61: Five fast facts about the Hall of Fame wide receiver and all-time touchdown leader.* CBS Sports. https://www.cbssports.com/nfl/news/jerry-rice-turns-61-five-fast-facts-about-the-hall-of-fame-wide-receiver-and-all-time-touchdown-leader/

Deion Sanders. (2024, April 11). Wikipedia. https://en.wikipedia.org/w/index.php?title=Deion_Sanders&oldid=1218338699

Dempsey, T. (n.d.). *To be a good field goal kicker you have.* Quote Catalog. Retrieved April 14, 2024, from https://quotecatalog.com/quote/tom-dempsey-to-be-a-good-fi-D7By4G1

Didinger, R. (2020, April 5). *Didinger: Tom Dempsey's career was more than just one memorable field goal.* Philadelphia Eagles. https://www.philadelphiaeagles.com/news/didinger-tom-dempsey-career-was-more-than-just-one-memorable-field-goal

Donahue, B. (2020, September 22). *The life and career of Deion Sanders (complete story).* Pro Football History. https://www.profootballhistory.com/deion-sanders/

Donahue, B. (2022a, February 12). *The inspirational life and career of steve gleason (story).* Pro Football History. https://www.profootballhistory.com/steve-gleason/

Donahue, B. (2022b, October 23). *The life and career of Jim Kelly.* Pro Football History. https://www.profootballhistory.com/jim-kelly/

Donahue, B. (2023a, January 23). *The life and career of Roger Staubach (story).* Pro Football History. https://www.profootballhistory.com/roger-staubach/

Donahue, B. (2023b, August 20). *The life and career of Tom Dempsey.* Pro Football History. https://www.profootballhistory.com/tom-dempsey/

Drew Brees. (2020, March 27). Biography. https://www.biography.com/athletes/drew-brees

Drew Brees. (2024, April 12). Wikipedia. https://en.wikipedia.org/w/index.php?title=Drew_Brees&oldid=1218622832

Drew Brees biography. (2024). Ducksters. https://www.ducksters.com/sports/drew_brees.php

The Editors of Encyclopaedia Britannica. (2020). Tom Brady. In *Encyclopædia Britannica.* https://www.britannica.com/biography/Tom-Brady

The Editors of Encyclopaedia Britannica. (2024, March 26). *Kurt Warner.* Encyclopedia Britannica. https://www.britannica.com/biography/Kurt-Warner

The Editors of Encyclopedia Britannica. (2019). Walter Payton. In *Encyclopædia Britannica.* https://www.britannica.com/biography/Walter-Payton

The Editors of Encyclopedia Britannica. (2024). Peyton Manning. In *Encyclopædia Britannica.* https://www.britannica.com/biography/Peyton-Manning

11 surprising facts about Kurt Warner. (2023, October 6). Facts.net. https://facts.net/celebrity/11-surprising-facts-about-kurt-warner/

Fan, C. (2023, August 13). *46 facts about Peyton Manning*. Facts.net. https://facts.net/celebrity/46-facts-about-peyton-manning/

Fang, P. (2024, March 2). *42 Facts about Rob Gronkowski*. Facts.net. https://facts.net/celebrity/42-facts-about-rob-gronkowski/

Feb. 24, 1985: Jim Kelly throws for 574 yards with Houston Gamblers. (n.d.). Buffalo Bills. Retrieved May 12, 2024, from https://www.buffalobills.com/news/feb-24-1985-jim-kelly-throws-for-574-yards-with-houston-gamblers-14962653

15 fascinating facts about Jim Kelly. (2023, October 17). Facts.net. https://facts.net/celebrity/15-fascinating-facts-about-jim-kelly/

Fish, M. (n.d.). *Pat Tillman timeline*. ESPN. Retrieved April 27, 2024, from https://www.espn.com/espn/eticket/story?page=tillmantimeline&redirected=true

Fitzgerald, L. (n.d.). *Larry Fitzgerald quotes*. The Dallas Morning News. https://www.brainyquote.com/quotes/larry_fitzgerald_664436

40 facts about Michael Strahan. (2023, August 22). Facts.net. https://facts.net/celebrity/40-facts-about-michael-strahan/

Gleason, S. (n.d.). *Steve Gleason quotes*. BrainyQuote. https://www.brainyquote.com/quotes/steve_gleason_545995

Gronkowski , R. (n.d.). *Rob Gronkowski quotes*. BrainyQuote. https://www.brainyquote.com/quotes/rob_gronkowski_857408

Guttmann, A. (n.d.). *Jim Kelly*. Encyclopaedia Britannica. Retrieved April 14, 2024, from https://www.britannica.com/biography/Jim-Kelly

Hahn, J. (2021, January 29). *From his hatred for coffee to his early bedtime: 9 things you didn't know about Tom Brady*. People. https://people.com/sports/super-bowl-2021-tom-brady-little-known-facts/

Hurricane harvey relief efforts. (n.d.). Justin J. Watt Foundation. https://jjwfoundation.org/hurricane-harvey-relief-efforts/

The inspiring story of Tom "the bomb" Dempsey. (2022, December 14). Sports History Network. https://sportshistorynetwork.com/football/nfl/tom-the-bomb-dempsey/

J. J. Watt. (2024, March 21). Wikipedia. https://en.wikipedia.org/w/index.php?title=J._J._Watt&oldid=1214802685

Jerry Rice. (2024, April 7). Wikipedia. https://en.wikipedia.org/w/index.php?title=Jerry_Rice&oldid=1217673405

Jerry Rice - stats, retirement & facts. (2021, November 12). Biography. https://www.biography.com/athletes/jerry-rice

Jerry Rice biography: NFL football player. (2024). Ducksters. https://www.ducksters.com/sports/jerry_rice.php

Jim Brown. (2024, March 27). Wikipedia. https://en.wikipedia.org/w/index.php?title=Jim_Brown&oldid=1215875469

Jim Kelly. (2012, August 2). Greater Buffalo Sports Hall of Fame. https://www.buffalosportshallfame.com/member/jim-kelly/

Jim Kelly. (2024, April 12). Wikipedia. https://en.wikipedia.org/w/index.php?title=Jim_Kelly&oldid=1218500394

Jim Kelly - trivia. (n.d.). IMDb. Retrieved April 14, 2024, from https://www.imdb.com/name/nm0446486/trivia/

John Madden. (2018, June 27). Encyclopedia.com. https://www.encyclopedia.com/people/sports-and-games/sports-biographies/john-madden

John Madden. (2024, April 10). Wikipedia. https://en.wikipedia.org/w/index.php?title=John_Madden&oldid=1218288315

Katsampiri, A. (2018, November 21). *Michael Strahan: 18 facts about the former athlete*. Useless Daily. https://www.uselessdaily.com/sports/michael-strahan-18-facts-about-the-former-athlete/

Kelly, J. (n.d.). *Jim Kelly quotes*. BrainyQuote. https://www.brainyquote.com/quotes/jim_kelly_873830

Kurt Warner. (n.d.). Pro Football Hall of Fame. https://www.profootballhof.com/players/kurt-warner/

Kurt Warner. (2024, April 6). Wikipedia. https://en.wikipedia.org/w/index.php?title=Kurt_Warner&oldid=1217604753

Kurt Warner: Career retrospective. (2023, October 4). Yardbarker. https://www.yardbarker.com/nfl/articles/kurt_warner_career_retrospective_100423/s1__38062976#slide_1

Lakritz, T., & Kalnitz, M. (2024, February 11). *18 things you may not have known about Patrick Mahomes*. Business Insider. https://www.businessinsider.com/patrick-mahomes-things-to-know-2021-2

Larry Fitzgerald. (n.d.). Sportskeeda. https://www.sportskeeda.com/nfl/larry-fitzgerald

Larry Fitzgerald. (2024, March 15). Wikipedia. https://en.wikipedia.org/w/index.php?title=Larry_Fitzgerald&oldid=1213786692

Larry Fitzgerald biography. (n.d.). OSDB. https://www.osdbsports.com/nfl/players/larry-fitzgerald/biography

Madden, J. (n.d.). *John Madden quotes*. BrainyQuote. https://www.brainyquote.com/quotes/john_madden_158609

Mahomes, P. (n.d.). *Patrick Mahomes quotes*. BrainyQuote. https://www.brainyquote.com/quotes/patrick_mahomes_972709

Manning, P. (n.d.). *Peyton Manning quotes*. BrainyQuote. https://www.brainyquote.com/quotes/peyton_manning_769472

Manning, P. (2022, February 9). *Peyton Manning*. Academy of Achievement. https://achievement.org/achiever/peyton-manning/

McChesney, D. (2023, August 22). *40 facts about Michael Strahan.* Facts.net. https://facts. net/celebrity/40-facts-about-michael-strahan/

McGreal, C. (2009, September 15). New book describes Pat Tillman as increasingly disillusioned with Iraq war. *The Guardian.* https://www.theguardian.com/ world/2009/sep/15/pat-tillman-iraq-book

McLaughlin, E. C. (2017, September 26). *Pat Tillman: 5 things to remember.* CNN. https://edition.cnn.com/2017/09/26/us/pat-tillman-5-things/index.html

Michael Oher. (2021, September 16). History and Biography. https://history-biography. com/michael-oher/

Michael Oher. (2024, March 25). Wikipedia. https://en.wikipedia.org/w/index. php?title=Michael_Oher&oldid=1215475316

Michael Oher facts. (n.d.). SoftSchools. https://www.softschools.com/facts/biography/ michael_oher_facts/3437/

Michael Strahan. (2021, April 20). Biography. https://www.biography.com/athletes/ michael-strahan

Michael Strahan. (2024, April 13). Wikipedia. https://en.wikipedia.org/w/index. php?title=Michael_Strahan&oldid=1218735625

Michael Strahan Facts for Kids. (2024, February 10). Kids.kiddle.co. https://kids.kiddle.co/ Michael_Strahan

Miller, C. (2022a, June 6). *10 things you didn't know about Rob Gronkowski.* TheSportster. https://www.thesportster.com/facts-about-rob-gronkowski/

Miller, C. (2022b, July 23). *10 things NFL fans should know about John Madden.* TheSportster. https://www.thesportster.com/nfl-john-madden-facts-trivia/

Most 400 yard passing games in Super Bowl. (n.d.). StatMuse. Retrieved May 12, 2024, from https://www.statmuse.com/nfl/ask/most-400-yard-passing-games-in-super-bowl

Most receiving yards in A single game in Super Bowl history. (n.d.). StatMuse. Retrieved April 17, 2024, from https://www.statmuse.com/nfl/ask/most-receiving-yards-in-a-single-game-in-super-bowl-history

Most seasons with 20 or more sacks by A player. (n.d.). StatMuse. Retrieved May 12, 2024, from https://www.statmuse.com/nfl/ask/most-seasons-with-20-or-more-sacks-by-a-player

Most wins by A QB in their first 9 seasons. (n.d.). StatMuse. Retrieved May 11, 2024, from https://www.statmuse.com/nfl/ask/most-wins-by-a-qb-in-there-first-9-seasons

NFL passing touchdowns single-season leaders. (n.d.). Pro Football Reference. https://www. pro-football-reference.com/leaders/pass_td_single_season.htm

NFL: Understanding the social significance of America's favorite sport. (2023, March 10). The Intelligencer. https://www.theintelligencer.net/news/2023/03/nfl-understanding-the-social-significance-of-americas-favorite-sport/

Norman, J. (2018, January 4). *Football still Americans' favorite sport to watch*. Gallup. https://news.gallup.com/poll/224864/football-americans-favorite-sport-watch.aspx

Oher, M. (n.d.). *Michael Oher quotes* . BrainyQuote. https://www.brainyquote.com/quotes/michael_oher_808782

1-36: facts on Drew Brees. (n.d.). New Orleans Saints. https://www.neworleanssaints.com/photos/1-36-facts-on-drew-brees-14788984#79b72aa1-f177-4cb2-840f-b3b97c6cefce

Ott, T. (2020, July 28). *Russell Wilson*. Biography. https://www.biography.com/athletes/russell-wilson

Pat Tillman. (2024, April 13). Wikipedia. https://en.wikipedia.org/w/index.php?title=Pat_Tillman&oldid=1218674848

Pat Tillman - Cool Facts. (2022). Studocu; Studocu. https://www.studocu.com/en-us/document/university-of-kansas/principles-of-biology/pat-tillmen-cool-facts/53253026

Pat Tillman Biography. (2017). TheFamousPeople. https://www.thefamouspeople.com/profiles/pat-tillman-10903.php

Pat Tillman quote. (n.d.). A-Z Quotes. https://www.azquotes.com/quote/812641

Patra, K. (2020, July 6). *Chiefs, Patrick Mahomes agree to 10-year, $503M extension*. NFL. https://www.nfl.com/news/chiefs-patrick-mahomes-agree-to-10-year-contract-extension

Patrick Mahomes. (2024, April 11). Wikipedia. https://en.wikipedia.org/w/index.php?title=Patrick_Mahomes&oldid=1218455960

Patrick Mahomes biography. (2021, February 16). Biography and History. https://biographyandhistory.com/patrick-mahomes-biography/

Payton, W. (n.d.). *Walter Payton quotes*. BrainyQuote. https://www.brainyquote.com/authors/walter-payton-quotes

Peyton Manning. (2024, April 12). Wikipedia. https://en.wikipedia.org/w/index.php?title=Peyton_Manning&oldid=1218638775

Piccotti, T. (2014, April 2). *Deion Sanders*. Biography. https://www.biography.com/athlete/deion-sanders

Piccotti, T. (2021, February 22). *Patrick Mahomes*. Biography. https://www.biography.com/athletes/patrick-mahomes

Readmikenow. (2023, August 6). *NFL legend: Tom Dempsey*. HowTheyPlay. https://howtheyplay.com/team-sports/NFL-Legend-Tom-Dempsey

Remembering Pat Tillman at Arizona State: A great Sun Devil, a greater man. (2024, April 22). College Football Network. https://collegefootballnetwork.com/remembering-pat-tillman-2024/

Rice, J. (n.d.). *Jerry Rice quotes*. BrainyQuote. https://www.brainyquote.com/quotes/jerry_rice_434405

Rice, N. (2021, January 28). *From his love of ketchup to his pro athlete dad: 7 things you didn't know about Patrick Mahomes*. People. https://people.com/sports/patrick-mahomes-things-you-didnt-know/

Rizzo, W. (2023, October 25). *7 things you didn't know about Deion Sanders*. 2aDays. https://www.2adays.com/blog/7-things-you-didnt-know-about-deion-sanders/

Rob Gronkowski. (n.d.). National Today. https://nationaltoday.com/birthday/rob-gronkowski/

Rob Gronkowski. (2024, April 13). Wikipedia. https://en.wikipedia.org/w/index.php?title=Rob_Gronkowski&oldid=1218790345

Rob Gronkowski bio & career accomplishments. (n.d.). FOX Sports. https://www.foxsports.com/personalities/rob-gronkowski/bio

Rob Gronkowski has the most receiving touchdowns by a tight end in a season, with 17 touchdowns in 2011. (n.d.). Statmuse. https://www.statmuse.com/nfl/ask/what-are-the-most-receiving-tds-in-a-season-by-a-tight-end

Roberts, C. (2020, January 16). *16 little known facts about Drew Brees*. TheThings. https://www.thethings.com/16-little-known-facts-about-drew-brees/

Roger Staubach. (n.d.). Encyclopaedia Britannica. https://www.britannica.com/biography/Roger-Staubach

Roger Staubach. (2021, October 4). Wikipedia. https://en.wikipedia.org/w/index.php?title=Roger_Staubach&oldid=1214538592

Roger Staubach quotes. (n.d.). BrainyQuote. https://www.brainyquote.com/quotes/roger_staubach_142241

Rolon, C. (2023, October 10). *14 mind-blowing facts about J. J. Watt*. Facts.net. https://facts.net/celebrity/14-mind-blowing-facts-about-j-j-watt/

Russell Wilson. (2024, April 12). Wikipedia. https://en.wikipedia.org/w/index.php?title=Russell_Wilson&oldid=1218640351

Russell Wilson facts for kids. (n.d.). Kiddle. https://kids.kiddle.co/Russell_Wilson

Ryan. (2023, January 11). *Dream big and work hard: The legacy of JJ Watt*. Greater than the Game. https://greaterthanthegame.org/dream-big-and-work-hard-the-legacy-of-jj-watt/

Sanders, D. (n.d.). *Deion Sanders Quote: "If you look good, you feel good. If you feel good, you play well. If you play well, they pay well."* QuoteFancy. Retrieved April 14, 2024, from https://quotefancy.com/quote/1656809/Deion-Sanders-If-you-look-good-you-feel-good-If-you-feel-good-you-play-well-If-you-play

Sandler, T. (2023, February 9). *5 fun facts about Patrick Mahomes*. Fangirl Sports Network. https://fgsn.com/5-fun-facts-about-patrick-mahomes/

Santos, L. (2022, June 21). *10 fun facts about retired Bucs tight end Rob Gronkowski*. WTSP. https://www.wtsp.com/article/sports/nfl/buccaneers/rob-gronkowski-career-facts/67-7d69f9a5-d578-4aaf-b3ef-b86b5c1defbc

Schulz, L. (2024, March 4). *11 enigmatic facts about Jerry Rice*. Facts.net. https://facts.net/celebrity/11-enigmatic-facts-about-jerry-rice/

Seaman, M. (2024, March 2). *37 facts about Tom Brady*. Facts.net. https://facts.net/celebrity/37-facts-about-tom-brady/

Shapiro, M. (2018, December 30). *Drew Brees breaks his own completion percentage record*. Sports Illustrated. https://www.si.com/nfl/2018/12/30/drew-brees-new-orleans-saints-single-season-competion-record

Silver, M. (2015, September 16). *The unbelievable life of J.J. Watt*. NFL. https://www.nfl.com/news/sidelines/the-unbelievable-life-of-j-j-watt

6 rare Michael Strahan facts you were never aware of! (2022, May 19). Daily Hawker. https://www.dailyhawker.com/entertainment/6-rare-michael-strahan-facts-you-were-never-aware-of/

16 intriguing facts about Roger Staubach. (2023, October 7). Facts.net. https://facts.net/celebrity/16-intriguing-facts-about-roger-staubach/

SportsDay Staff. (2019, March 29). *10 things to know about Roger Staubach: From serving in Vietnam to playing catch with a young Bill Belichick*. Dallas News. https://www.dallasnews.com/sports/cowboys/2019/03/30/10-things-to-know-about-roger-staubach-from-serving-in-vietnam-to-playing-catch-with-a-young-bill-belichick/

Stackpole, K. (2023, May 19). *Jim Brown dies at 87: 32 facts about 32, from NFL legend's milestones to post-football achievements*. CBS Sports. https://www.cbssports.com/nfl/news/jim-brown-dies-at-87-32-facts-about-32-from-nfl-legends-career-milestones-to-post-football-achievements/

Steve Gleason. (2024, March 3). Wikipedia. https://en.wikipedia.org/w/index.php?title=Steve_Gleason&oldid=1211697348

Steve Gleason facts for kids. (2023, December 28). Kiddle. https://kids.kiddle.co/Steve_Gleason

Strahan, M. (n.d.). *Michael Strahan quotes*. BrainyQuote. https://www.brainyquote.com/quotes/michael_strahan_644462

Superstar Artists. (n.d.). Gronk Beach Las Vegas 2024 Big Game Weekend. Retrieved May 12, 2024, from https://gronkbeach.com/artists/

Suzuki, H.-A. (2023, October 26). *8 mind-blowing facts about Walter Payton*. Facts.net. https://facts.net/celebrity/8-mind-blowing-facts-about-walter-payton/

Ten fun facts about Jerry Rice. (n.d.). 10 Facts About. https://www.10-facts-about.com/jerry-rice/id/1239

Ten fun facts about John Madden. (n.d.). 10 Facts About. Retrieved April 14, 2024, from https://www.10-facts-about.com/john-madden/id/1232

Ten fun facts about Larry Fitzgerald. (n.d.). 10 Facts About. https://www.10-facts-about.com/larry-fitzgerald/id/1253

Ten fun facts about Roger Staubach. (n.d.). 10 Facts About. Retrieved April 14, 2024, from https://www.10-facts-about.com/roger-staubach/id/1230

Ten reasons why people love the NFL. (n.d.). The Bookshelf: Exploring EdTech and Cognitive Psychology. https://blogs.cornell.edu/learning/ten-reasons-why-people-love-the-nfl/

32 facts about 32: The numbers that defined Jim Brown. (2024, April 14). Cleveland Browns. https://www.clevelandbrowns.com/news/32-facts-about-32

Tom Brady. (2023, August 30). Biography. https://www.biography.com/athletes/tom-brady

Tom Brady. (2024, April 8). Wikipedia. https://en.wikipedia.org/w/index.php?title=Tom_Brady&oldid=1217916673

Tom Dempsey. (2024, January 22). Wikipedia. https://en.wikipedia.org/w/index.php?title=Tom_Dempsey&oldid=1197897381

Tuohy family to remove references to Michael Oher being adopted in Blind Side legal battle. (2023, November 29). *The Guardian.* https://www.theguardian.com/sport/2023/nov/29/tuohy-family-michael-oher-lawsuit-adoption-references

12 fun facts about Seahawks quarterback Russell Wilson. (n.d.). Seahawks. https://www.seahawks.com/news/12-fun-facts-about-seahawks-quarterback-russell-wilson-116212

The ultimate Brown: A timeline of Jim Brown's life. (2023, May 19). Cleveland Browns. https://www.clevelandbrowns.com/news/jim-brown-life-timeline

Waddle, M. (2024, March 4). *25 Astonishing Facts About Larry Fitzgerald.* Facts.net. https://facts.net/celebrity/25-astonishing-facts-about-larry-fitzgerald/

Wallenfeldt, J. (2020). Patrick Mahomes. In *Encyclopædia Britannica.* https://www.britannica.com/biography/Patrick-Mahomes

Walker, A. (2017, October 4). *Peyton manning "humbled and honored" by statue dedication, number retirement.* For the Shoe. https://www.colts.com/news/peyton-manning-humbled-and-honored-by-statue-dedication-number-retireme-19506372

Walter Payton. (2021a). pro Football Hall of Fame Official Site. https://www.profootballhof.com/players/walter-payton/

Walter Payton. (2021b, April 15). Biography. https://www.biography.com/athlete/walter-payton

Walter Payton. (2024, April 13). Wikipedia. https://en.wikipedia.org/w/index.php?title=Walter_Payton&oldid=1218698599

Walter Payton facts for kids. (2023, October 27). Kiddle. https://kids.kiddle.co/Walter_Payton

Walter Payton NFL man of the year award. (2024, April 16). Wikipedia. https://en.wikipedia.org/w/index.php?title=Walter_Payton_NFL_Man_of_the_Year_Award&oldid=1219162677

Warner, K. (n.d.). *Kurt Warner quotes.* BrainyQuote. https://www.brainyquote.com/quotes/kurt_warner_952303

Watt, J. J. (n.d.). *If you want to be remembered as great, if you want to be a legend, you have to go out there every single day and do stuff.* BrainyQuote. https://www.brainyquote.com/quotes/j_j_watt_811256

Weyer, M. (2022, September 24). *10 things NFL fans should know about Walter Payton.* TheSportster. https://www.thesportster.com/walter-payton-nfl-trivia-chicago-bears/

What makes American football so popular? (2023, January 23). CFP. https://www.collegefootballpoll.com/news/what-makes-american-football-so-popular/

White, L. (2019, February 20). *5 things you didn't know about Russell Wilson.* Beliefnet. https://www.beliefnet.com/entertainment/sports/5-things-you-didnt-know-about-russell-wilson.aspx

Whyte, I. (2023, August 16). *All you need to know about the blind side's Michael Oher.* TVovermind. https://tvovermind.com/michael-oher-facts-things-you-didnt-know/

Woodworth, H. (2023, August 9). *48 facts about JJ Watt.* Facts.net. https://facts.net/celebrity/48-facts-about-jj-watt/

Made in the USA
Monee, IL
23 November 2024

71034247R00090